AN AMISH JOURNEY TO FORGIVENESS

Discovering My Anabaptist Roots and Destiny

Benjamin Girod

iUniverse LLC
Bloomington

An Amish Journey to Forgiveness
Discovering My Anabaptist Roots and Destiny

ISBN: 978-1-4759-6319-9 (sc)
ISBN: 978-1-4759-6318-2 (hc)
ISBN: 978-1-4759-6317-5 (ebk)

Library of Congress Control Number: 2012921856

iUniverse books may be ordered through booksellers or by contacting:

iUniverse LLC
1663 Liberty Drive
Bloomington, IN 47403
www.iuniverse.com
1-800-Authors (1-800-288-4677)

Printed in the United States of America

iUniverse rev. date: 08/08/13

Also by Benjamin Girod
"The Amish Church, Will it Stand the Test of Judgment" **1992**
"Rekindling the Anabaptist Flame" **2000**
Im Fire Getaufed" **(German) 2003**
"Baptized by Fire" **2006**

To David, Josephine, Samuel, and Peter. Your incalcuable suffering and incrediable triumph over the giants of disease and pain continue to inspire me to press forward in the joy of the Lord. I shall always thank God for you, with love and deep affection.

"Put the swing where the children want it, the grass will grow back."
Amish Proverb

Table of Contents

Foreword

Within the pages of this book, you will find a remarkable and unusual story of Amish life. This story reflects Ben Girod's painstaking social and spiritual journey. What God allowed to transpire in his personal and social life over many decades, prepared him for what was to unfold later in life, in the spiritual realm. This story chronicles life with his wife Barbara, and a family of nine children; as well as life as an Amish Bishop.

Ben's responsibilities as a church leader were manifold as he dealt with the predominant and inherent traditions of the Old Order Amish church. Ben himself was once among the strictest sect of them all—the Swiss Old Order Amish in the vicinity of Berne Indiana.

A truly divine encounter with God brought an unknown peace with unspeakable joy to the lives of Ben and Barbara Girod. This was soon to be followed by misunderstanding and rejection by family, church members, and leaders alike, ultimately ending in excommunication from their respective district. Devastated and confused, and unable to understand why all this was happening, and with no one to turn to, they turned to the Lord in search of some meaning and purpose in it all. As time unfolded, they began to understand that God was allowing such persecution and suffering, to draw them closer to Him. Over the years, unsettling church experiences continued to unfold, which in the end, left them feeling forsaken, abandoned, and alone.

Through this saga of suffering God was preparing them for what they were to ultimately walk-in, with respect to their impact upon the Church at large. God in His goodness and mercy had opened their eyes to the place and purpose of the Ministry of Reconciliation. The message of reconciliation up until this time was largely unheard of, and rarely taught throughout the global Church Body. It was during this season that the ministry of Anabaptist Connections was born—a ministry and message that the Church universal desperately needs to hear, incorporate, and teach—a message declaring that there is a better way, a way that leads by way of the Cross; denying oneself, and dying to our own will, for the sake of others. This message needs to go out across the globe, if we are to find hope to be reconciled with the Body of Christ at large, in light of the deplorable and fragmented state we find ourselves in today.

God has used Ben and others like him, to bring about an awareness of the pressing need for healing and reconciliation throughout the Body—an awareness that is now prodding hearts throughout the globe. Knowing that Christ will not return for a fragmented Bride, but one that is whole; Ben and Barbara have willingly walked through much travail to see this wholeness carried out.

May the God of Peace receive all honor, glory and praise through the telling of this story, and may He continue to lead those of you that He has called accordingly, to hold fast the torch of reconciliation; lighting fires of hope, repentance, with renewed relationships throughout the body of Christ, that the world may then see and know that His people are marching forward with one heart and mind, serving each other, as Christ served His first disciples. And in and through this demonstration, may they too believe on Him.

Ray Yoder is a pastor and leader among the Mennonites, was co-founder of the Kootenai Valley Mennonite church near Bonners Ferry, Idaho.

Preface

With the outgoing tide of the Church Age, making way for the incoming tide of the Millennial Kingdom Age, I witness the unveiling of many precious treasures in the form of saints who have withstood unspeakably fierce and fiery trials over many decades—saints who have become so dead to the world as the result, that they have truly become other-worldly in their devotion to Christ Jesus. Such the treasure I have found in my precious friend, Amish Bishop Ben Girod.

I have long marveled at the widespread positioning and posturing for notoriety within the mainstream Church in this country. Very few who fall prey to this behavior have an understanding of what it means to fulfill an authentic apostolic role in this age. Truth be known; those who walk in such a role are the last to claim such. For they have broken-free from the lures of fanfare, and have become as the "dregs of the earth," despised by many, and often uncomely in countenance. It seems to me that a number of pivotal figures within the pages of scripture come to mind at this point.

It is rare that a Believer endure a lifetime of scorn and suffering, without also succumbing to deeply rooted bitterness and spiritual despondency as the result, in what should rather be the Golden Years—a final chapter of life laced with peace and joy. Ben Girod has handsomely emerged as a champion of the faith, having walked upon fiery coals of suffering for much of his life, to now carry a mantle of humility and authority to the Amish Nation, and beyond.

For those who've but a cursory knowledge of the Amish, and Anabaptists in general; I invite you to open the eyes of your heart as you read the pages which follow, that you may in turn readily recognize the unfolding of a precious chapter of Church History as we know it.

I have enjoyed for many years, overhearing the comments of those unfamiliar with Amish culture, as they pay cursory visits to densely populated Amish districts. Uniformly, it is the quaint introversion, quietness, gentleness and humility that visitors speak of. Largely unknown to visitors, is the profound purpose brewing within the Amish Nation—a purpose which is now gracefully approaching a divine appointment internationally—not unlike the grace and beauty of a bride making her way forward in a wedding ceremony.

The book in your hands was penned by the contemporary torchbearer of such the move; a man who, for much of his life, was "the voice of one crying in the wilderness" of deathly legalism and oppression. Within his lifelong saga, highlighted much of the time by deep suffering, Ben refused to permit the roots of bitterness to take root within the soil of his heart. To the contrary, he, as well as the jewel represented by his wife Barbara, rather chose to permit the course of their pain to fashion the unmistakable trademarks of humility, and spiritual authority.

It was as I was fasting and meditating some years ago upon the life histories of Menno Simons and Jakob Ammann, Anabaptist pioneers of what would ultimately become the Mennonites and Amish respectively; that I was given a divine glimpse into the hearts of these men. Though space will not permit such, I will yet offer that both of these men bore passionate pursuits for holiness and intimacy with the Lord—equal only to their passion to impart the same to their brethren. As I have continued to study Amish history over several years, I have come to recognize the passing of a generational baton—a baton once held by Jakob Ammann—and a baton which is now gracefully carried by a growing number of Anabaptists. Among them is Ben Girod as he embraces the upward call, pressing-on beyond barriers of suffering and persecution which most would have yielded to long ago.

I take emotional license at this point to express something to you, Ben, which may perhaps seem ill-fitted within the forward of a book. Nonetheless, it is with tears that I repeat to you that I love you; I count your friendship precious and priceless; and that trudging through the trenches of warfare within the work of the ministry with you has been one of the highest honors of my life to date.

Your trench-mate,
David Davonport

Acknowledgements

Writing has always been one of my passions and I've used what skills my Amish education provided me to write as often as I could. Writing my life story is another matter altogether, so I looked to my precious friends for assistance. David Davenport worked long on the initial manuscript and Micah Smith on the final edit. These men were able to take my Amish style of writing and turn it into a priceless gem, greatly magnifying the message of my life and heart throughout the book. I marveled at their dedication, together with much pains-taking time and efforts to see the hidden message within my heart formed and revealed within these pages. I will never be able to repay them, neither would they ask anything in return. God is their reward!

Years ago when I started writing, my original goal was to write a colorful story about my wife's life, growing up in an Amish family, on the backside of the Pennsylvania hills. But as time passed, I was prompted by the Lord to weave the fabric of both our lives, as we were drawn towards an unknown destiny—To her, with our nine children, I am forever indebted for their lifelong support!

Ben Girod

Introduction

Like the country roads I traveled as a boy, my life has been a journey of unique and often unexpected twists and turns, especially for a conservative Amish man. The most unexpected turn in my life's road has been one of forgiveness with my Anabaptist family. By family, I am not merely referring to my biological family, although, that aspect of restoration is certainly true in my story. I am also referring to my Amish, Hutterite and Mennonite family.

The Anabaptist movement is almost 500 years old, dating back to the Christian reformation in Europe. Growing from what became known as the protestant reformation, early Anabaptists were given this title because they viewed infant baptism as having no force or binding power because the infant was not cognitively able to make a confession of faith in Christ. Finding confirmation in the Scriptures led them to a re-baptism of Christian believers as adults. This act resulted in a heavy persecution of Anabaptists in the sixteenth and early seventeenth centuries by Europe's state Church, both protestant and catholic.

One example is Hans Schlaffer, a former catholic priest, who joined the Anabaptist movement. On December 5, 1527, Hans was arrested, interrogated, tortured and two months after his arrest, he was executed. His crime? That he no longer believed or practiced infant-baptism. Hans stated that according to the Bible, a man had to "hear, understand, believe, and receive" God's word before being baptized. In his heart and mind, this constituted Christian baptism. Hans was well known for his prayer life and his passion in calling others to prayer. On the night before he was executed, he wrote a letter to his brothers and sisters in Christ, which included a prayer with these final words,

> "Eternal Father! We pray that You will send workers into Your vineyard; for the harvest is great, while the laborers are few. We pray for all those who carry Your gospel throughout the whole world, that You will strengthen them with the power of Your holy spirit, that in them all the terror of man may be quenched and that they will not renounce Your Word through fear. "Sustain us in Your Holy Name, and let us not wander away from You, fountain of living waters, that we may hold fast to the true faith firm unto the end."

Today, there are many different streams, representing many different traditions among the Anabaptists. My birth and upbringing was among the most strict and conservative, even among the Amish. I grew up in a deeply segregated Amish community near Bowling Green, Missouri during the decade of the 1950's.

I became a horse and dairy farmer in this isolated community of roughly one hundred families. As a child, my father Peter served as bishop of two church districts in the northern part of our community, while Jacob J. Miller was bishop of the two southern districts. We lived in a world completely our own, largely set apart and removed from our English neighbors, or any other culture for that matter. Even our business was performed among our community, inaccessible from others, whether in town, the market place, construction site or in the local sawmills. This environment created the culture, in which I was raised, eventually got married, began a family and lived for many years in relative obscurity.

My life was filled with the responsibility of caring for handicapped siblings, working on the farm and tending to the immediate needs of my wife and children. I never once dreamed there was any other life than the one I was living in my Amish culture and community. While using horse and plow in our fields, I remember watching with wonder, airplanes crossing the sky, high above our farm. With only my imagination, could I dream about the people and places carried on the wings of those planes. But God was working behind the scene. Often while plowing in the fields with a draft of horses, or milking cows by hand in the barn, the Lord was calling me for a life of service, even before I was aware of it. His call was shaped and forged in the fires of my own need, as I read, studied and learned our Anabaptist history.

Typical for an Amish man, I possessed no credentials or degrees, which are standards of measure in normal American life. I absorbed little more than a 6th grade education and that from a remote Amish parochial school. My admiration for people with an academic education has been life long and something, which I have always wished to achieve. Now I understand that it was in the isolation of Amish anonymity and responsibility of family care that the Lord taught me many lessons of spiritual significance, which would later serve His plan and purposes. I knew nothing of this at the time but had a real hunger to know Christ and gain spiritual understanding and to see the world through God's eyes.

In the beginning of the Reformation countless Anabaptists were murdered for their faith. Others incarcerated, living on meager amounts of stale bread and contaminated water. Many Anabaptists were left in abject poverty by the state authorities, stealing and confiscating their homes and livelihoods. During the reformation, these early Anabaptists enjoyed a growing relationship with Christ, which gave them the energy and persistence to carry on. This kind relationship glue was very similar to what held the early believers together as recorded in Acts 2:42-46(KJV). This strength, rooted in the bonds of deep fellowship, enabled them to rejoice on their way to being burned at the stake in 1600 Europe.

These stories served to fuel my fire to learn. I read the Martyrs Mirror, the writings of Menno Simons, with many other books about our history. God used my spiritual hunger, Anabaptist culture and a desire to study our history to shape my future. When I learned about these historical accounts, I began to understand God's call on my life. God was using our history to speak to us. And the call was clear; Seek forgiveness and reconciliation with others to complete the original Anabaptist vision of fulfilling the Great Commission. Matthew 28:18-20 (KJV)

At home, and in our churches, we sang these sad melodies that spoke of our forefathers sufferings. They are mournful songs from the "Ausbund Hymnal" (perhaps the oldest hymn book in the world, still in use). Each songs stanza describes the deep suffering and anguish these early Anabaptists endured. For this reason, the Amish people are draped and infused with a martyr's spirit, one of deep sadness and melancholy. As I grew, being exposed more and more to this sorrow, it puzzled me because I did not understand our Church history. More troubling was how and why the suffering, now centuries past, still manifested such brokenness, among the Anabaptists.

I now understand how the seclusion of Amish communities has a trickle down affect upon families and members. Although each Amish community appears secure and strong to outside observers, in reality there was very little concern for any other Amish communities. We often suffer alone as a community, as a family and as a person. These dynamics all played a significant role in my life, as God prepared me for a ministry of forgiveness. This is miraculous because we are a divided people and I often wondered how we would all meet the Lord in this fragmented condition. Initially, I naively believed each movement would be found right in God's eyes in the end, and that somehow we would all become one in heaven.

Not until the Lord opened my eyes to the stark reality of my own deplorable, spiritual condition, did I began to understand that our traditions as Anabaptist people, fell far short of a growing, personal relationship with Christ Jesus. Speaking from my own experience and observations, I understood that our traditions had slowly eroded and replaced biblical truth accompanied by nurturing a relationship with Jesus. Although many of our traditions are intrinsically good and worthy of generational practice, it dawned on me that Jesus' own words had largely come true among us as the Amish people.

Matthew 15:3 (KJV) And my heart was humbled with an urgency that compelled Barbara and I to call on the Lord for mercy.

When our journey of forgiveness began in 1981, little if nothing did I understand of the remarkable, yet painfully difficult path, which stretched out before us. We felt all alone because we were alone; we had no one, family or friend, to turn to for advice, counsel, or comfort for several years. I rejoice now, because it was in these years, God revealed Himself to us with great care and compassion. He helped us understand the Bible and how it fit into our lives with living hope and faith. Before we could call others to restoration, reconciliation and forgiveness, we had to experience God's grace in our own hearts and everyday living.

I recognize that I have no platform of authority upon which to stand nor do I promote any sense of self-righteousness. From our first steps, we had no idea of the global impact this ministry would have nor did we begin to guess what far-reaching impact on so many people, from two continents. No one is more surprised than I am.

I simply tell my story with the hope that other fellow travelers will be encouraged to join me in God's great story of redemption. And it always begins with forgiveness. These chapters are about our forgiveness journey but it is my sincerest hope you are encouraged to recognize signposts of forgiveness as you travel your path.

These are but a few of the life lessons I have learned with my wife Barbara and our nine children. Together we sought to restore relationships through identificational repentance among our Anabaptist family, as modeled by the prophet Daniel.

Daniel 9:4-6 (KJV)

Or as Moses did when he stood in the gap for his people, *Israel*.

Numbers 14:11-20. (KJV)

Join me, as we pursue with God, "...the final restoration of all things, as God promised long ago through His holy prophets."

Acts 3:21. (KJV)

Chapter 1

BEGINNINGS ON SAM HILL

My wife, Barbara grew up in the 1950's among the beautiful hills and valleys of east central Pennsylvania, in Snyder County, where the wide, rock strewn Susquehanna River meanders nearby. Raised in a family of eleven children, five boys and six girls, Barbara was the fifth child born into a deeply, religious Amish culture.

Their farm was nestled on top of a high plateau where five roads from all directions led to the top of the hill with valleys round about. This hill, given the name Sam Hill, provided Barbara's family with an impressive vantage point of the farm fields, which bordered dense forests. Wildlife such as deer, occasional bear, raccoons, woodchucks, rabbits, quail, pheasants and squirrels were in abundance. The region was filled with an endless variety of birds and wild flowers, which filled the air with their delightful songs and the fields with brilliant color and sweet fragrance.

The old country school she attended was two and one half miles to the east, set in a green valley. Typically, Amish children attend school for eight years. And for each of their eight years, Barbara and her brothers and sisters walked the two and half mile trail from her home to the school house and back. Every day they carried with them old-fashioned 1-gallon pails containing their lunches, which generally consisting of apple butter sandwiches, an egg sandwich and a jar of milk and occasionally they enjoyed chocolate milk.

Growing up, Barbara was extremely shy and timid. Her quiet and unassuming ways often caused her to be left out as the other children played and interacted on the playground. Nevertheless, She would entertain herself with a keen connection to nature and wildlife. During the daily walks to and from school, she learned to identify many species of songbirds, which were abundant in her unspoiled region of Sam Hill. Along with study of nature, she discovered she had an artistic gift and whenever time allowed, Barbara would venture into the woods, find a suitable place to sit down on a tree stump and begin sketching the scenes before her. Sometimes a Red squirrel would become her object. Other times, wild flowers such as Rhododendrons, Black-eyed Susans and wild Daisies would come alive in her sketches. Other times, a songbird or the distant valleys and mountains were sketched out with great detail. Because she was such a friend of God's creation, wildlife seemed to have no fear in her presence.

Until recent years and the expansion of technology and media, people living outside Amish communities knew little of Amish life. We Amish wanted it that way and we worked hard to keep and maintain our privacy. On the other hand, the Amish were also isolated from the rapid advances of the modern world. Our joys and our sorrows were confined within the communities where we lived.

Sorrow and sadness entered Barbara's sheltered life at age fourteen, when her mother passed away. Barbara was deeply shaken by the death of her mother. It was a traumatic loss, taking her into an unknown and indescribable time of grief and pain and a broken heart.

Aside from the emotional heartache, her mother's household responsibilities were assigned to Barbara. This was a tremendous time of stress and pressure that a girl her age, generally knew nothing about. Most of her older brothers and sisters had grown up and left home by this time, which required that she take care of the younger children. This included cooking meals, doing laundry, mending and tailoring of clothes, washing dishes and many other things inherent with raising a family. Every night for some time, because of the loss of her mother, she would cry herself to sleep. One night in a dream, Barbara heard her mother calling her name. As she continued to call her she woke up, sat bolt upright as she heard her mother's voice calling out to her. In an amazing way, the dream was accompanied by a deep healing and peace, which filled Barbara with a comforting acceptance of the loss of her mother. From that moment on, Barbara shouldered the weight of her responsibility with supernatural grace.

The Amish have always been industrious and self-reliant people, with a strong work ethic. During the time she was growing up, many farmers in central Pennsylvania raised tomatoes for commercial sale. Late summer into autumn found gardens and farms lush with mature fruits and vegetables. The smell of late summer grasses and foliage was pungent and intoxicating. The brisk air meant it was tomato-picking time. Along with other Amish youngsters, Barbara would pick tomatoes for neighboring farmers during harvest. It was backbreaking work, often on their hands and knees, picking from morning 'till night. The Amish young people harvested endless rows of tomatoes, filling hampers, one after another. Many became expert pickers, often picking over two hundred baskets a day. Even so, they had fun, from time to time, taking breaks when an occasional tomato throwing battle broke out among them. This helped unravel the monotony with some fun and laughter.

Later in the fall, the much anticipated apple harvest would begin. Snyder County was filled with apple orchards and the harvest was a popular destination for people to help increase their income. This afforded what seemed like, endless opportunities for apple picking by Amish and Mennonite boys and girls. People traveled from all over the country to pick apples in this famous apple-growing region.

Then there was the nationally known cantaloupe. The rare Snyder County shale soil helped produce a quality and sweetness of these melons, which was unequalled. They were grown, packed and sold by Titus Hoover Enterprises, sent to stores all over the eastern seaboard. There were also the numerous sawmills, and pallet shops all over the county. Work was to be had, for those who wanted to work. Barbara and her family grew up working hard season after season with not so much as a thought about it; this was Amish life.

By age eighteen, Barbara had grown and blossomed into an extraordinarily beautiful young woman. She continued her practice of walking alone along wooded trails, deep in the forest. She was drawn to the beauty of the woods with its mountain laurels and various flowers. Always, there was the challenge to identify some rare bird. Her spirit grew in the presence of God within the isolated beauty of this unspoiled region of Pennsylvania. She could dream in these woods, and dream she did, of a greater purpose for her life, a purpose that would someday reach beyond her lovely Sam Hill and Snyder County. She dreamed of her future and becoming a nurse, longing to share God's compassion with others. As she continued to dream, the Lord would gently guide her forward, and into His incomparable plan for her life.

Chapter 2

THE RISK OF REACHING OUT

The Amish community where Barbara lived was small, largely
isolated from the greater region Amish districts in Pennsylvania.
The main reason for this was because her church had reached out to
help a smaller church in the area, which was not a part of the Old
Order Amish. This resulted in Barbara's Church community being
rejected. But being small and isolated wasn't completely adverse since
the youth in her community developed a strong and genuine bond.
Families did not use automobiles for transportation or electricity
for light or heat in their homes. Although no modern conveniences
could be found in the community it did not hinder the youth from
having great times of fun and developing meaningful relationships
with each other. On weekends they would go camping, hiking far
into the woods to cabins they had built. Groups of boys and girls
could be seen walking the roads together on Sunday afternoons,
while jesting light heartedly and playing. Then they conclude Sunday
with a worship service, where there was always lot's of singing.

The fall hunting season was a big highlight. They would hunt
for big game such as deer and bear, as well as smaller game like
turkey, pheasants, rabbits and squirrels. Not only did this provide
a much-needed high value protein for families, there was a spirited
and energized competition among the tightly knit group. Using their
hunting and woods savvy, each member used their skills to harvest
the largest deer or bear for the winter's store.

As winter set in, the woods became overlaid with deep snow, which launched the sledding season. What delight this winter wonderland brought to the children and young people in the community. The long roads leading into the valley were often heavily laden with ice and snow during the winter. And with reckless abandon, they competed with each other, flying along the twisting, icy tracks, cheeks red from the frosty cold. Rarely did the sledding season end without some serious accident and injury. Yet, there was the unrelenting pursuit to possess the fastest sled with the shiniest, most glazed runners. It was the thrill of a lifetime to lead and win a sled race on Sam Hill.

In the fall of 1969, when Barbara was nineteen, along with brothers and sisters, she traveled west to visit friends and relatives in some distant Amish communities. For the first time in her life, she ventured beyond the borders of her familiar world.

But I am glad she did. It was on this excursion that Barbara and I met for the first time.

Because of her quiet and delicate nature, she was very hesitant of connecting with someone of the opposite sex. She felt more at home in the Pennsylvania woods near Sam Hill. Many other young men pursued her attention, and with little success, including me. Try as I might, Barbara would not be rushed into any premature relationship and I often felt hopeless of ever gaining the trust and love of her heart. Even so, I felt God was guiding our lives together. Though I could not see it in the moment, there was a stirring, an indefinable hope, that our lives were linked by God's design. Touched by her gentle spirit, I was left totally undone by her exquisite beauty. Barbara, on the other hand was content to wait upon God's guidance until she was at peace in the matter. Not until she received an unmistakable word of divine confirmation, would she give her word and move ahead in any kind of courtship. For me, the waiting was excruciating and intolerable but I was persistent. She had captured my heart and I had decided I would not give up. Finally after some time, Barbara responded to me with a "yes". I was beside myself with happiness because it felt like a flood of joy and peace washed over me.

Our four-year courtship was a long-distance romance, nurtured through a weekly exchange of letters. I lived in Missouri, which was a great distance from Pennsylvania, for a young Amish couple courting. Every September, after the crops were in, I would travel from Missouri to Pennsylvania to visit her. Our courtship forged a strong bond of trust and love as we sat and shared our hearts and dreamed of the future. We had one big problem though. Barbara made it known that she would never leave her beautiful Sam Hill. At the same time, I was committed to family responsibilities, which made it impossible for me to have the freedom to move to Pennsylvania. This was the first of many tests of our commitment to one another.

Amish communities do not institutionalize their elderly or relatives in poor health. For generations, it has been the kinship duty of the immediate family to provide and give them care. I shared in the daily responsibility of taking care of four of my siblings who were wheelchair bound. This was a huge, demanding task, not one I despised but faced as a challenging impasse. Barbara and I agreed to continue our long distance courtship but I knew that was not the permanent solution. One day I was emotionally wrestling with the situation and I received news that she would be willing to come join me, if I would promise to take her back to Pennsylvania at the first opportunity. As you can imagine, I made her this promise with pure delight and joy! We began to make plans for her move right away. Again, we would face tests, which would prove our love and make us strong for God's future plan.

Chapter 3

LIVING OUT MY NAME

Following the biblical example, our parents thoughtfully choose given names in Amish culture. Each name contains depth of meaning and driving influence for lives. My given name is Benjamin. You can read in the book of Genesis how the name Benjamin is connected with the anguish of Rachel, when she gave birth to her son Benoni. But like most names, the name Benjamin contains more color and definition than merely "anguish", it also means; "the son of my right hand". This is the name Jacob gave his son and it has a deep significance and meaning for me personally. Yes, my birth was hard and painful for my mother, yet, she knew, I was destined by Father God for His greater purposes.

My beginnings were typical for a Swiss Amish boy, completely foreign to the people and the surrounding towns near my community in Berne, Indiana. My parents had ten children, and I was number eight, as we Amish are given to large families.

The Swiss Amish communities of Adams, and Allen County, Indiana were tight-knit and isolated even among the greater Amish cultures nationwide. At age seven, I began first grade, where I attended the first newly built Amish school on my father's farm.

My father was a bishop in the church and became a forerunner in developing the first parochial schools in the Swiss Amish community. I completed my first two grades in the school building built by my father and my oldest brother David was my teacher. The State of

Indiana had strict academic standards and David was required to go to Indianapolis with a scholar for each grade to test their learning skills. Each grade passed above average. Within two years however, my father received such bitter opposition, both from within the church, and from local authorities, that he had to shut the school down. This was a very troubling time when the persecution finally came to a head after some local thugs burned the School building to the ground during the night.

This was my world, the only world I knew until I grew to the age of ten, when my parents moved our family to Bowling Green, Missouri in the spring of 1954. We quickly settled on a 160-acre farm nestled in the center of another traditional Amish community. Unknown to me, or any of us for that matter, the way we lived and how I grew up had little resemblance to neighboring towns. My world more closely resembled seventeenth century Europe than twentieth Century America. Compared to the post World War II baby and industrial boom, our Amish community was extremely disconnected and primitive. The outside world was outside and that is the way we kept it and the way we thought it should be.

Every child has challenges when growing up. I've learned that the challenges are not what prevents one from growing but rather how we respond to the challenges before us. The most debilitating challenge I faced was chronic earaches and infections, which cruelly plagued me throughout my growing years. And I had no idea it was developing into a serious and often fatal condition. My misery and illness worsened as a serious depression clung to me from age twelve to sixteen. My dad struggled too, not knowing, nor understanding my problem. Although he tried to help, he was at a loss what to do and at times helplessly threatened to take me to an institution for treatment.

Like other families, our challenges were compounded by daily responsibilities that needed attention no matter what other problems we faced. We all had a job to do and one of my jobs was gathering the eggs from the hen house. One day, my mom asked me to go gather the chicken eggs and I while I was busy searching each hen's nest, my mind suddenly exploded with the crazy notion that I would not live past the age of twenty one years old. Imaginations can run amuck and mine did when I concluded that the twenty-one eggs, I gathered, represented the number of years I was to live on earth. Try as I might, I could not unravel this fearful notion. It wrapped itself around my head like a serpent. Then, simultaneously and with sudden shock, I was gripped with a dark, foreboding, and oppressing terror. It was awful and the gloom that overshadowed me took me to what felt like, the pits of hell, as I stood there holding tightly to that basket of eggs. I even thought I heard a voice confirming this terrible personal prophecy. I now look back on this horrifying episode and realize that in spite of what evil forces were working to halt God's plan for my life, that Jesus is greater than anything we face. And He promised to never leave us and He certainly never left me. His presence was most warmly experienced through my mother's faith and assurance. As a boy, mother was the only person I dared share the fears and torment I was experiencing during these four years of private pain. Never once did she forsake me. I will always remember with love and affection her gentle, giving spirit, constantly sharing and spreading sunshine in my agonizing world. One of the ways she lifted my emotions was her keen ability to fill our house with singing. Like her Swiss parents, she was an expert singer, with a wonderful talent for yodeling, which I inherited. The English word Yodel has its roots in the German word Jodeln, which means to "utter the syllable Yo". Her lovely, clear voice would lift the fog of depression from the darkest day with high, low, high, low pitch singing. God wonderfully used her attention and love to bring hope into my life. To this moment, my fondest thoughts are often fixed on my mother's love and support.

With surreal sequence, it seemed my premonition was true for by my twenty-first birthday, I was admitted to our local hospital, near death. My ear infection had become so dreadful; it had penetrated into my brain, causing a perpetual dizziness often called Vertigo. For two weeks, I went through the most excruciating hell imaginable. I could not live and I could not die, nor did my family expect me to survive this ordeal. Even my doctor later told me that he doubted I would survive because all the statistics were against me. But God had a plan for my life and I did survive. Since then, I have endured numerous surgeries on both ears and I still suffer some of the effects of chronic ear infections. But I rejoice for the calling God has given me because I now understand that His purposes always prevail for those who will follow Him.

Growing up on our farm, I learned agriculture the old fashioned way, using real horsepower. We did all the farming with horses. We used the horses to help us sow wheat and oats. The horses enabled us to thrash the grain, haul the hay from field to the barn, and plant and harvest corn. There was no modern machinery to be found on the Girod farm. Everything was accomplished by hand, using our horses and what a big help they were.

We also milked twelve cows by hand, as well as raising and selling feeder pigs. All this hard work was but the normal course of life for us. We never once thought it out of the ordinary because this was all we knew in Amish life.

There were also wonderful times of recreation, where our family joined other Amish families for outings and gatherings. It was strictly unthinkable and entirely off-limits to seek or pursue any interactions with people outside the Amish community. This greatly reduced the sphere of our world and confined us to a very limited understanding what lay beyond our communal lifestyle. Yet, it never dawned on us that we were being deprived of anything, or missing life in the outside world. We were generally content with our shielded life as Amish children. It was later, as we grew that we began to understand the Amish way of life contains both positive and negative aspects.

My father was born November 11, 1906 and became a nationally known Amish bishop. To me, however, and most importantly, he was the hero of my life. He was a strong man with great leadership qualities; his influence reached many Amish communities throughout the land. His preaching was always practical, straightforward and to the point and his care for the churches was equaled by his good shepherd's heart. He shunned the singsong tone in his preaching that many are noted for among the Amish, choosing to simply communicate the truth of God's word.

What I remember most vividly about him was his steadfast love for us, his family. On February 13, 1970, he and mom had worked hard, making homemade laundry soap in a large iron kettle outside. This was a common practice among the Amish. It was a typical frosty February day. That evening, I recall how they had finished their day's work and came up to the porch to sit down and rest for a few minutes.

We all noticed at once that something was wrong with my dad.

As I watched him, I could tell he was not feeling well. I started to walk across the porch where he was sitting, as he let himself down on the cement porch. I quickly caught him in my arms. Kneeling down, I worked to cradle him and in the blink of an eye, he was gone. My dad died in my arms. It happened so swiftly! One instant he and mother were talking and the next, he was gone. For a few moments, I just stared at him as the realization of his death began to send the effects of shock throughout my body. Time seemed to stand still. In the background, I could hear my mother weeping. Then as the shock of loss and sorrow spread to my brothers and sister, they began to weep too. Without words, my brother Jake came over and knelt beside me. Together, we lifted dad in our arms and carried him over the threshold of front door, laying him on a bed in the house. I realized, that Jesus, whom dad loved and served all his life, had also carried dad across heaven's threshold.

Three days later Amish leaders, communities and families gathered around us, as we celebrated the home going of Peter Girod.

Chapter 4

MY BROTHER'S KEEPER

I believe God uses life experiences both good and negative to help shape us for His plan and purposes. As one man said, "God never wastes a pain". Is it easy? No, I would never suggest that life's pressures are easy but I have found that with every pressure, God has a promise to be discovered. Now looking back, I can see that He used three older brothers and one older sister, to help shape me. They were afflicted with a condition medically termed, muscular dystrophy. This genetic disorder causes the muscles to atrophy and lose their tone. Their condition was first noticed at about the age of six and very slowly, yet persistently their conditions worsened. David, Josephine, Samuel and Peter suffered greatly. There are no words to describe how they suffered or how their suffering impacted our family.

In the spring of 1954 dad took my oldest brother David to a chiropractic sanitarium in Denver, Colorado, where after six months, he had excellent results. Because of the success, we hoped to take all four of them to Denver for the same treatment. Because Dad had invested large sums of money for their care, he did not have the financial resources to send the other three. Our hopes were delayed but not denied when in 1966, the dream to take my siblings to Denver for treatment was revived when I was twenty-two years old. The task became my God-given vision and mission. First, I worked to engage the rest of the family to help make this dream become a reality. All that summer we planned the various aspects of this monumental undertaking, especially the financial difficulties involved. Most of the family saw this mission as an unattainable dream. But I didn't and I couldn't let it go because of glowing reports David brought back from his first visit.

Incredibly, on October 29, 1966, along with my youngest brother Jake and youngest sister Emmy we finally took all four of my siblings to Denver. This was not without the help of our drivers, Beryl and Elisabeth McConnell.

Now I look back on that season of my life and had I known what lay ahead in the following five months, I would never have attempted the feat. But isn't that how God works? He simply lays an impossible task before us and all we have to do is trust Him to pull it off. After all, if we can do it in our own strength and ability, with our own resources, it probably isn't God's plan. Mark 6:30-44 (KJV) And this undertaking ended in a most glorious way for all of us, and in a way that only God could bring it about.

Here's how it happened. After I paid the drivers their fees, the examination fees and the first week of treatments, I was out of money, which left me in a sudden shock. At first a pall of gloom shrouded my mind because humanly speaking our situation was utterly desperate. In retrospect, I now know that I had vastly underestimated the monumental costs of hospitalizing my brothers and sister. Even though the hospital gave each of them a sizable discount, provided me with free room and board for helping out at the hospital, the costs were nevertheless prohibitive. I could not possibly absorb such cost, even with help from the rest of the family. Every night in the privacy of my dormitory room, I began crying out to the Lord in desperation. After a number of weeks, our debt had climbed into thousands of dollars, an exorbitant sum in the mid 1960's. I struggled with the decision to stay, which looked foolish, or leave, which was also an appalling thought.

My brothers and sister needed the treatment but I had no money and no way that I knew of to raise such funds to pay the bill. One evening after the work at the hospital was finished, I lay on the floor of my room praying. I admit it was an agonizing moment, where

I desperately cried out for God to help us, to deliver us from this impossible dilemma. I can only relate to you what happened as I prayed. Suddenly, it seemed the floor under me began shaking, not a little, but violently. I jumped up to my feet surprised at first and a bit frightened. This was very unusual. But then in the same moment, I was filled with the peace of God. Somehow I knew His presence was there, in the room with me. My tradition provided no frame of reference for this experience but it was so real, it wasn't long before I laid down to rest and was sound a sleep. Sometime during the night, I had an unusual dream, like a vision. In the dream, I saw a sudden supply of money coming to our family. It came in large amounts and did not diminish until I saw myself paying off all of our debts to the hospital. And amazingly, the money continued pouring in to my family throughout the dream.

When I woke up, the morning sun was shining brightly in Denver, with clear blue skies over the Mile High City. At first I was disappointed because nothing had changed, however, in the following month, the dream became a reality precisely as I had seen it. God laid it on the hearts of hundreds of Amish people across the nation to send in donations on our behalf. Individual people sent us financial gifts. Churches, communities and, even businesses sent money to us. The support kept coming and coming for many weeks. I shall forever thank God and be grateful to my beloved people for their generosity. Just as in the dream God had given me, the finances continued to pour in miraculously. In our time of desperate need, people responded to God's prompting and helped us through a humanly impossible situation. Even the owners of the hospital gave us two weeks free of charge. Our relationship with this hospital continued for the next twenty-five years, as we would return for more treatments. I will always remember their generosity with great fondness and appreciation.

We remained in Denver another five months, where my brothers and sister made great strides in physical healing and spiritual growth. We met and befriended other patients from all over the country; even many of the doctors and nurses became our good friends, enveloping us with friendships that lasted for many years.

Thousands of miles from home and all alone, I am amazed at how God helped us. Many people under these circumstances would never have taken such responsibility without fortifying themselves with some sort of financial security. I innocently, but blindly, stepped into the unknown not having the capacity to comprehend the magnitude of such an undertaking in a large city. Is this what one would perhaps call blind faith? I do not know, but I do know how God sovereignly helped us through this painful but ultimately rewarding school of faith. The sufficiency of heaven met us in the very moment we were sinking into financial ruin. I shall never forget God's saving power in that critical time of need, how He reached down and saved us right on time.

By the grace of God, the treatments they received at Spears hospital enabled my three brothers and one sister to live approximately twenty years beyond their predicted life expectancy. By God's mercy and the compassion of many people, I watched them all live to a ripe age.

Chapter 5

FORGIVENESS MUST BE GIVEN

Thursday, September 6, 1973, Barbara and I became husband and wife at her childhood home on Sam Hill. I cannot describe how happy I felt to become her husband. After all, I had waited four years, which seemed like an eternity, plus one more day.

Our wedding was typical for our Amish heritage and simple by modern standards, but a profoundly joyous and happy occasion. The central Pennsylvania day was spectacularly bright and clear, with just a hint of autumn in the air. We gathered for the ceremony and when I saw Barbara for the first time her beauty left me speechless. She was radiant in her Amish dress, as our family gathered around to share in our marriage vows.

We had no idea of how our new life together would be one of shared burdens and blessings, lovely dreams and bitter disappointments. Yet, God was with us and His grace was more than enough to grow us through each trial and test we would face. At last, we were together!

After our marriage, we remained at her father's home, where I worked in his pallet shop. All that winter I nailed pallets by hand, earning a good sum of money to begin our new life. Then, in early March we loaded her furniture and personal belongings on a truck and left Sam Hill for our new home in Missouri.

Sometimes it is the most difficult decisions in life that produce the greatest rewards. When Barbara made the decision to leave her family farm on Sam Hill and marry me, she helped set into motion a series of steps, which God would use for our future ministry together. We discovered little by little, that to obey the Lord's leading, even if we did not understand it, invariably brings divine favor, protection, and untold blessings. God's ways are amazing, mysterious and always higher than our ways.

The following summer, with my brother Jake's help, we started building a small but sturdy house near my parents. The house was completed November 1, 1974, a month before our first child, Esther was born. It was here on this 160-acre farm that we lived and farmed with my brother Jake for the next ten years. All the fieldwork was done by "horse" power. We had increased our milking herd to fifteen cows, which we continued to milk by hand every morning and evening.

David, Josephine, Samuel and Peter, incapacitated in wheelchairs, remained under our care and their needs had to be met day and night. This was a seven day a week, twenty-four hours a day responsibility. With all the daily chores on the farm, this became exhausting and very time consuming. But we loved them and their care was a labor of love. I rarely chaffed under its burden. Nevertheless, because of the perpetual care required for them, there never was much time for recreation and rest. As one can imagine, these demands stretched Barbara and me to our limits. Especially Barbara, for she was living in completely new surroundings, adjusting as a newly wed, learning the ropes in a new community, plus the new environment of our local Amish church. At times, it was quite a trial for her delicate nature for every direction she looked there was change and adjustment. She often sought the refuge and safety of our modest house rather than socializing with those in the community. Some People in the community misunderstood Barbara's shy nature and unassuming ways.

Barbara often dreamed about, and at times wistfully spoke to me about returning to beautiful hills of Pennsylvania someday. On rare occasion, and when time permitted, we would take an outing, which required long drives with our horse and buggy. Our buggy rides would often take us to a nearby lake, where we could be still and quiet, which was a wonderful way to remove the stress from our demanding lives. Numerous times during our first ten years in Missouri, we would drive all the way to the waters of the mighty Mississippi river and have a picnic on its banks. This was some 20 miles from our home and a rather long, one-day, round-trip with horse and buggy. These were our special times to share and be alone together. We immensely treasured these times, for they were rare indeed. Much of our ten years in Missouri was lived, quietly raising our family and working our farm.

Chapter 6

REVIVAL AND RESISTANCE

A s husband and wife, Barbara and I longed to know Jesus. We wanted more than the form and tradition of our Amish upbringing. Not that all tradition is harmful or unnecessary. We identified with the Apostle Paul, when he wrote, "that I may know Him", (Phil. 3:10) and we were not quite sure how to travel the path of knowing God, because many of our Amish customs and traditions are healthy and good for the family and community. Although Jesus was indeed preached throughout Amish culture, He was an abstract figure, held at a distance and apart from the center of our faith. Jesus was not preached or pictured as a present, living Savior and such messages always left a void in our hearts, which we did not know how to fill.

But the hunger for God and a spiritual fire continued to burn causing us to reach out to other Christians beyond our Amish church community. This was ardently frowned upon, so, we learned to do our searching quietly and discreetly. In time, we discovered other Amish, who were seeking Jesus as the "Living Water" to satisfy our spiritual thirst. Unable to resist our desire to know Him, we began to meet with others to secretly study the bible. This sparked a spiritual fervor within the group, causing others to eagerly and quietly join in. The longing to study the bible was so intense that these studies often went right through the night, 'till 4 and 5 o'clock in the morning. Revival fire began to break out with such intensity that it was reminiscent of the historical events birthed in Switzerland in1525. Because the church forbade bible study, the secret gatherings continued to meet usually in complete darkness, so we would not be detected.

Because our gatherings were growing and we met often, we expected the Church leaders would eventually discover our bible study. We could not gather in hiding like this forever. And as we suspected, we soon learned that spies had been planted among us to apprise the leaders of our bible studies.

Soon after, the persecution broke out in full force. Although we were committed to follow Jesus, fear and anxiety were unrelentingly pursuing our peace. Some of the leadership and community became hostile and vengeful, intent to quench this newfound life out of us. Here is where Amish tradition has veered off the path of a living, growing relationship with God in Christ. The very air over the whole community became charged and electrified by false accusations and gossip to the point that many considered us to be heretics even though they had no substance to their accusations. Our crime? Studying the Bible and worshipping God outside the exact format and structure of the weekly, designated meetings. What were the leaders afraid of in our bible studies? What religious tradition covets most. They were afraid of losing control.

Very quickly, an avalanche of false charges came pouring in; It reminded me of the condemnation and cruelty I had read about of our early Anabaptist forefathers as they often hid in the night from the authorities.

The resistance to our desire to seek the Lord, gained momentum within the community and the tactics were predictable. First, we were individually forced into isolation; being terrorized and often disgraced. Then, we were brought before church councils to be interrogated, being made an open spectacle before the entire Church. Finally and under threat, they implied that we are being sanctimonious, violating the sacredness of the Amish church and their traditions.

I'll be the first to say that tradition can be a good and life giving practice if the traditions are seen as roots of faith nurtured in the soil of mutual trust and healthy relationships. However, traditions cannot assume first place over knowing Jesus (John 3:3) or growing together in Christ. (Ephesians 5)

When the Schrock's began embracing Christ, they quickly became outcasts sending shock waves throughout the Amish world. A lot of folks were astonished that one of their hero's was embracing what they termed in our German tongue, "*fremda glauben*", meaning a heretical faith. This certainly seems outlandish to people on the outside looking in but maintaining the status quo of five hundred years of tradition is the most important objective, not the serving the people but the traditions.

During this time trusting relationships developed between those who continued to gather. Two significant people in our lives were Glen and Ida Yoder. Glen was a gifted leader, who contagiously led us to Jesus and His message in the Bible. Joe and Rachel Schrock were also our close neighbors. In trustful abandon, we stood together under this intense pressure. Persecution has a way of knitting hearts together and we were no exception. We became intensely loyal to each other under this heavily charged atmosphere. However, since there was no escape, and as the pressures mounted, the group finally disbanded and went in different directions.

Some members of the groups eventually left the Amish community joining other Churches, who had opened their arms to them. By this time, we were not welcome among any of the Amish communities in the States; instead, there was the threat of ultimate Amish discipline of shunning and excommunication.

Even some of our own family members turned against us, creating an extreme situation and emotional anguish. Since we lived and worked together everyday, our day to day, lives were filled with increased family tension. It was unbearable. Since childhood, I had experienced a close and trusting relationship with my brothers and sisters. Now, a dark gloom hung over us as we tried to cope with this awkward situation. Although my heart ached over the situation, I understood their predicament within the community. As I wrestled with this impasse, my conscience tore at me. On the one hand I did not see how we could remain in the community and on the other I could not consider forsaking my considerable responsibilities with them.

The pressure of internal family tension, coupled with the external pressures coming from the church, there were moments when I felt as if I were being crushed between solid-rock. I could not move forward or backward. Church tradition would no longer tolerate the group Bible studies or me. They saw this as a deviation of the faith of our Amish roots and history. They considered the deviation as being rooted in my insistence that we have the freedom of informal bible study in groups. Within our community this was a huge violation of our traditions. Since a Bible study like this was beyond the control of typical and standard church meetings, we were refused and condemned. In this season of pain, we called out to the Lord and He answered us. Although we felt hedged in, we were soon to learn that when the way appears impossible, God makes a way. He always does.

Chapter 7

The Crucible of Hope

Little by little, God filled us with hope as we grew in Christ and experienced the freedom we were reading about in the Bible, but not without real and daily challenges.

For Barbara, trusting God each day was a matter of child-like faith, which came simply for her. Not so for me, as I wrestled with the daily challenges in the community and in my own soul. But we persisted and walked together in seeking the Lord for understanding and guidance.

He answered in a most unusual manner. What I am about to share, I have no way of logically explaining because we do not fully understand or comprehend it ourselves. I can only share with you and relate what happened one night in the midst of our dilemma.

It was around 2am, Barbara got up for a drink of water. Walking into the kitchen, a brilliant, bright light surrounded her. The illumination was so sudden and overwhelming that it caused Barbara to bow down to the floor shielding her eyes.

It is important for you to know and keep in mind how unusual this is for anyone, especially we Amish who do not have electricity in our houses. To say, she was overwhelmed is understating the awe she experienced in what she later described as a holy moment. Completely shaken by the encounter, she hurriedly returned to our bedroom, waking me from a sound sleep.

At first, I was unable to grasp what had happened as she tried to explain to me the unusual phenomena. For the rest of the night we quietly discussed her extraordinary encounter and what it could possibly mean to us. As the days passed with growing tension, we came to realize that the light was God's assurance of His presence in our lives. He was guiding our steps in the light of His protection and plan. Oh, what joy this gave us as Psalm 119:105 declares; "Thy word is a lamp unto my feet, and a light unto my path." (KJV)

This was significant because of the growing and severe tension around us. The contrast between God's peace inwardly and the strain outwardly was incredible. Our entire family was embroiled in the caldron of a severe community shakeup. Nerves were on edge and ready to snap at the drop of a hat. Misunderstandings and relationship upheavals became constants in daily routines and responsibilities. On the one hand it looked like there was no way out toward reconciliation, yet the joy of the Lord was our strength!

For years following, we did not understand how the ancient strongholds of strife and divisions being manifested in our confined Swiss Amish culture, worked to destroy us.

Looking back on that painful time of distrust, I now realize, God was preparing us for the ministry of restoring relationships through forgiveness. 2 Corinthians, 5:18-21(KJV)

Before we left the community, I was prompted by the Lord to go to each of my brothers and sisters and ask for their forgiveness. At the time, this made no sense and seemed an unreasonable step to take, for I did not feel that I was at fault, perhaps even the opposite was true. Even so, I went to them, seeking forgiveness out of obedience, not because I understood it at the time. From this point in life, I began learning the art of obedience, often at the expense of logic, intellectually formed opinions and human understanding.

Beside our small house stood a giant oak tree, which stood like a sentinel and guardian over our home. I purposely had built our small house under this magnificent tree. The huge Oak canopy and branches were a haven for many types of birds that came to nest and sing their songs. We heard the warbled and varied shrills of Blue jays, Wrens, Mocking birds, Woodpeckers and many other species throughout the year.

One day, a flaming Red Cardinal decided he wanted to come inside our house. So, he began fluttering against the glass of the living room window. He did this day after day, and the days turned into weeks, and the weeks into months. It was such an odd occurrence. Every morning he fluttered next to the window to get in. Finally, the day came when we took pity on him. We carefully captured the beautiful, red bird and took some distance away from the house in order to convince him that his mission was elsewhere.

Immediately however, another bird took its place, wanting to come in.

The Bible tells us in Job 12:7-8 (KJV), that there are times God uses, even birds to teach us His ways. Finally, it dawned on us, that the Lord Jesus was using these birds to speak to us. In essence, we understood His message to us as:

"Let Me come into your hearts and in your home, and I will wash you clean with My blood. You shall be pure, and white as snow."

He was asking us for access and entrance, to more deeply inhabit our hearts and lives. God was preparing us for the next step of His plan and purpose. We knew the Lord, but the message was clear and very much like Ezekiel's vision of a river of life in the book bearing his name (Ezekiel 47:3-5). The vision pictures the possibility of going deeper with the Lord. At first, Ezekiel, steps into the river and is only ankle deep. Then he wades in up to his knees. Anyone who has ever slowly waded into the water of a cold mountain lake or river understands the sensation of going deeper. Next the water rises to his waist and finally he is over his head, swimming in the river of life. God wanted us to move deeper into His life and allow Him to move deeper in our lives.

Yes, Lord Jesus! we agreed, "take us deeper!" For the first time, in our lives, we were fully confident and filled with blessed assurance of our salvation. We began to trust Christ completely, in all things. We finally realized and got it, the Lord was not out to get us, and He was growing us into the image of His Son, Jesus Christ.

Chapter 8

Shaped for God's Purposes

People on the outside looking in cannot imagine how deeply Amish tradition is ingrained into the soul, from birth to death. This must be why the Lord shaped us with radical encounters, so we would know without any doubt that it was He, who was leading us. Now, I understand how the Biblical record re-enforces this tactic. God used a radical plan in Joseph by way of a Bedouin slave route to Egypt, Moses, through the burning bush and I cannot leave out Saul of Tarsus, knocked from his donkey in a brilliant light. There are many others and I certainly am not saying, I am a Moses or Saul, but I do know and appreciate that God had to use some radical tactics to get our attention and shape us for His purposes.

It was perhaps a week after Barbara encountered the Lord's light, that God had a radical encounter planned for me. I was busy working on the farm, when the passage in Romans 8, again came to mind. At the same time, and in this instant, the Holy Spirit suddenly immersed me, so deeply that it felt as if my natural faculties had completely left me. The Holy Spirit continued to surge through my heart and throughout my body. With this holy presence came the warm sensation of an unutterable peace in my heart, peace of unspeakable dimensions. It seemed that the presence of God completely enveloped me. Simultaneously, God gave me revelation of *Romans 8:24-25,* which I had studied numerous times.

> The Apostle Paul begins v-24 with these words, *"For we were saved in this hope"*

With supernatural clarity, God revealed to me that my hope of salvation was not a someday possibility but a present reality. The Bible says, "we were saved in this hope". I knew I had instantly been transformed in my mind and heart. The ecstasy of the moment knew no bounds; no earthly vocabulary could describe it, or compare with it. My wildest dreams, my deepest longings, my greatest hopes, or all that I ever desired on earth overwhelmingly flooded my soul at that moment, my finite mind could not grasp it, and it was beyond human reasoning. The joy of the moment followed me for a week.

The Amish continually stressed a doctrine of hope, partially founded upon *Romans 8:24-25 (KJV)*. This doctrine had, over many generations, been deeply implanted throughout Amish culture, imbibing our very DNA. Since the Amish do not believe in a present salvation, they always stressed the word "Hoffnung", meaning, "hope", which is hope to be saved when we die. For this reason I meditated upon, searched, and studied at length, this word "hope" for many, many years, in hopes of finding peace within its context and practical application for everyday life.

I had grappled with this elusive hope for so long, that I had long felt there was hidden within its concept, something that would one day reveal a deeper meaning and in turn fill the void deep within my heart. In the end, after all those years of searching I was not disappointed.

Being naive and ignorant, I had no words to describe what I had experienced, while working on the farm. There was nothing else in my Amish life and upbringing that I could compare with being born again (John 3:3) and having full assurance of salvation (Hebrews 10:19-25). Since I was inexperienced in such things, I thought this occurrence was the norm for every person coming to Christ alone for salvation. Only later, would I find out differently.

In fact, I now know most Christians come to know Him, in a far less dramatic way. However, our shared encounters with the Lord, there came a responsibility far beyond our ability to fulfill, in ultimately reaching out in global proportions to Anabaptist peoples from many nations, with a message of healing and forgiveness. This was no choice of ours, but Gods sovereign design for our lives.

For some time, only Barbara knew about my encounter with the Lord. And it required weeks for me to fully grasp what happened. One thing I know is that in November 1981, on our isolated farm nestled in northeast Missouri, I met the Lord and my heart was filled with hope.

On the one hand, I had no mentor to help me navigate the revelations. The spiritual climate within the Amish community was completely closed to a living relationship with Jesus. Going to Church leadership was out of the question. This only propelled Barbara and I to invest time together, praying, reading the Bible and trusting God to guide us. And on the other hand, we joyfully understood that we had been led on the first steps of what would become a colorful journey into God's future for us. With a new hope, a hope within the safety and presence of God, we stepped forward.

Just a day or two after this encounter, I was splitting firewood one evening from a woodpile we had close by the house. Some of the children were standing close by, ready to carry in the wood into the house, as I split it.

Like a bolt of lightening, a hawk shot past my face flying at the woodpile. Just before hitting it, the hawk turned, and shot straight upward toward the sky. This happened so fast that it me a few moments to figure out what I had just witnessed. What I discovered was the hawk had attempted to catch a dove, which I found in the woodpile, frightened but alive. I gently pulled it out and held it in my open hand. As I was holding it, the hawk was watching from a tree 200 yards away. Barbara and the children all excitedly gathered around me, petting the dove.

Again, God used a very dramatic and unusual event to speak to our hearts. We understood that the narrow escape of the dove was like our escape from the dark pit of fear. The talons of the hawk had just missed the dove and so, God had delivered us from the talons of destructive traditions. It was a seriously sober and hushed moment as I continued to hold the dove with the family surrounding me.

Then the dove flew away.

Barbara and I pressed on forward in our spiritual journey. We experienced the vibrancy and life of the Bible as we studied it together. We found new dimensions of application to everyday living. With this ongoing discovery came the filling of the deep void, which had for so long dominated our hearts. We had now discovered the true rivers of living waters for which we had been seeking for many years. With growing hunger we studied, searched, and absorbed the Word day and night, discovering truths and revelation upon revelation, and we simply could not get enough. There were times as we were studying, that I would have five or six different bible translations with several commentaries scattered all over the dining room table, searching out to the fullest meaning in each passage as we read and studied it. We did this in the secret privacy of our home, marveling how the Holy Spirit unveiled the mysteries of God during those moments. Even in our hostile surroundings, God filled us with His peace.

I also studied more deeply our Anabaptist roots and how our Anabaptist forefathers, whom we had so deeply eulogized and revered for entire generations, knew a genuine and growing intimacy with Christ Jesus. This troubled me because I saw how far we had drifted from this kind of communion with Christ. I love my Amish people and thank God for the rich heritage I have but it appeared to me that we had now perpetuated a lifeless religion, devoid of a personal relationship with Christ as Savior.

This revelation came with such shocking proportions that it left us asking deep and penetrating questions. Had our Amish and Anabaptist traditions replaced a living, growing relationship with Christ? Had our rules and rituals led us down a path full of dead men's bones? Are the words of Jesus, as recorded in the seven woes of Matthew 23 applicable to our current spiritual condition? Was God's judgment staring us in the face?

Like a flood, these questions and revelations filled our hearts and minds. In no way, did we feel or believe ourselves superior or apart from these questions, in fact, just the opposite, because we are Amish. These are our people, whom we love and thank God for even though they were treating us with great hostility and rejection. We continued to pray and study the Bible, not fully realizing that God in His mercy was divinely knitting within our hearts the burden of intercession for our people globally. We felt this for the entire Amish Nation. Though we had no one within the community or beyond with whom we could turn to for answers or for comfort, the Lord was with us and we simply placed the growing burden before Him. We knew He would reveal His way of redemption for our people and He did.

Chapter 9

THE SUFFERING OF SEPARATION

Predictably, spiritual unrest amplified in our churches as a desire for the deeper things in Christ continued to increase. The over flow of friction required my brothers and sisters to seek refuge in other homes, where some of them would live out the rest of their lives. This decision caused great emotional anxiety for us. Yet, somehow God's grace helped us endure these dark days of harsh realities. We knew they would not last forever and change was soon coming.

One of the methods God uses to get us to change is pain. If you hold your finger in a flame long enough the pain will reach a point where you will finally move your finger.

The pressure of opposition mounted, while we began to consider a change. For a long time, we prayerfully considered the idea of a move to the hills of Pennsylvania where Barbara was raised. The pain of the long struggles within the family and our immediate community finally compelled us to make the change Once the decision was made, we began the weeks of planning required for such a monumental move.

My youngest brother Jake, with his wife Sovilla, would take over the farm following the negotiation of an agreeable price. This included the dairy herd and all the farm machinery. The transaction was completed in March of 1983. However, we remained in Missouri another four months following the sale of our share of the farm. Although my brothers and sister had decided to move into other homes, I wanted to insure they were properly cared for and their needs would be met. Every day I would leave my house and walk and run over five miles, from home to home, where they each lived and apply massages and body manipulation. These physical techniques I had learned during our time at Spears Hospital in Denver. The Doctors taught me much in the line of chiropractic care, which I had used to help them for years.

The four-month delay also afforded me the opportunity to help Jake on the farm. We worked hard replacing the roof on their large horse and dairy barn. In this way, the summer days passed swiftly and before I knew the time to move to the Pennsylvania hills had arrived. For Barbara, this was a grand home going! We had recently bought a sixty-acre farm neatly nestled upon the crest of Sam Hill, within a mile from where she had grown up. Our hopes ran high and we could dream once again. We were excited about our beautiful farm we looked forward to a sanctuary for our growing family. I on the other hand was truly torn between a fresh start and leaving my family. From the beginning of our lives, we had known no other life than the one we shared in our father's house. The sense of loss was heart wrenching to the core of my being. This may not make sense to those outside the Amish-Mennonite culture, but in spite of the bitter strife that often takes place behind the scenes; the soul-ties within family members are nevertheless extremely binding.

In light of this, the closer the time came for us to leave the greater the tension grew between us, the atmosphere became charged, which was primarily expressed with a stark silence between us. There was not the usual jesting or idle talk, only waiting in dread for the inevitable separation. One bright spot, however, was one of my brothers decided to go along with us and make his home with us in the hills of Pennsylvania. This really softened the blow of the inevitable departure and separation we were all about to experience.

Once there, we anticipated our troubles to be over, little did we know however, what awaited us. God graciously kept these things from our knowledge.

Chapter 10

GUILTY AS CHARGED

Before we ever left Missouri, many people within the church in Pennsylvania had been communicating with us concerning our newfound faith in Christ. They were full of questions and inquiries about what we had experienced and what it all meant for us as Amish people.

Our arrival was met with eager anticipation by some people, others were doubtful and mistrusted our claims of salvation. There is an inherent spirit of fear in the Amish, especially in things we do not understand. This is never, more true, than when considering Biblical truth or the work of the Holy Spirit in a person's life. Jesus taught extensively on this subject in the Gospel of John chapters 14, 15 and 16 and in the book of Galatians chapters 3,4 and 5.

Moving day was set for August 15, 1983. This was the big day we were to load our belongings, together with Enos and Bertha Yoder on a semi trailer, bound for our new Pennsylvania home.

We all felt edgy and the atmosphere was mingled with both hope and fear.

Many people came by to help us with loading the truck, after which came the sad embrace and final goodbyes to our family. That evening we left my childhood home never to return. When you walk through this kind of emotional struggle, it is only natural to want peace and quiet away from the stress and pressures of life. I recognize that I elaborate on these emotions a great deal. But for a long time, this is how we lived and as people sometimes say, "We felt under the gun". There was the constant presence of human pressures, stress and friction, while the presence of God covered us, filled us and protected us. Like much of life, we lived between the tensions of blessings and battles.

Our hope and dream was to settle down in our new home in the hills of Pennsylvania, and to quietly raise our family, and for three years that is what we did. And it was wonderful. Of course, our desire to know Jesus and grow together spiritually never diminished. And over time, we began to form relationships with a group of recently born again believers who met to study the Bible. Dannie D. Troyer, a young deacon, was the leader of the group. We became friends and forged a close connection and friendship. Other friendships were made and we enjoyed the fellowship of many within our new church, many who, through initial encounters with me found new life in Christ, which I so eagerly lived and taught.

It would not be long until many in the church were gathering together many times throughout the week for fellowship and study of the Bible. There was great joy as we discovered life in Christ together and God helped us understand the Scriptures we were studying. In the following year many in the church joined-in and found this previously unknown peace, joy and freedom that is only found through intimacy with Christ.

But it was not long until the leadership in the church, who took a dim view of such activities, found this out. The momentum of salvation could not be stopped nor could it be ignored. The numbers of new Believers was swelling, while the troubles enlarged. It was amazing to watch the cycle happen all over again, which ended up in conflict between the new Believers and the Community leadership.

This time the conflict could not be contained within the local church, as it spilled out over all the Amish churches throughout the eastern states. It became so severe that within a short time the believers within the church began scattering in many directions. Although Amish churches are autonomous and stand alone, each is intrinsically connected to others. We often refer to ourselves as a nation and we are indeed a nation with language, religion and culture. In spite of ancient living practices in the modern world, there are lines of communication within the Amish Church that is faster than a Boeing 747. In a short time, the news had spread far and wide. Within the Amish system, there is no safe place for escape for those who come under the scrutiny of Church leadership. Consequently, the new believers leave, seeking out fellowship in various Christian movements.

But for my family, leaving the Amish church was not an option open before us. The Lord compelled us to stay; yet, we had no clue how our church membership would survive, if we remained. Why we were not allowed to leave the Amish at this time remained a mystery, we only knew we could not leave.

Honestly, we were deeply hurt again. First by the Pennsylvania Church rejection but especially so by the departure of the people with whom we had carefully nurtured to faith in Christ. Had we been able to follow them it would greatly helped along in the healing process. After many years, one of the men who left with his family came to me with a word of apology. He desired forgiveness for making such a hasty departure from the community and us, when we were all under such pressure to conform to Amish tradition. It was my joy to forgive him. Today, Amos and Rhoda Schwartz, along with their family carry a powerful testimony for Christ. Their tender and broken hearts speak volumes about how deeply they know Christ. (Philippians 3:10). The pain and rejection they have experienced in their lives has worked wonders in them. Their shining testimony is reaching distant lands and people with the good news of Jesus.

Once again, Barbara and I began to call out in prayer to the Lord for deliverance. We were in a very tight spot, not only our local church, but also many other Amish communities around the eastern seaboard. In a short time this turmoil expanded on a national scale. Only one family remained to stand with us. Being alone, and singled-out, we were vulnerable to attacks now from throughout the Amish system. Many wanted to see us expelled and banned. Leaders of various communities throughout the land came together, holding secret meetings, and dialoging as to how they should best deal with us.

This tension and turmoil spanned the duration of seven years, the combined years we spent in two different communities in Pennsylvania. Throughout all this time, I was never given a voice in my defense nor was I ever given any opportunity to testify of my faith to anyone, or to refute the false charges that were continually coming against me. The inflated charges multiplied with time, coming from every direction, and from Amish communities everywhere. I could not understand what was happening, I was hurting no one, nor was I resisting authority; I was not even in the ministry or officially preaching the Gospel. My crime seemed to rest on the evidence that men and women were coming to the knowledge of salvation.

In agonizing suspense we waited for the dreaded verdict to fall, which would ultimately come: "Guilty as charged!" This meant being shunned and excommunicated. Which, when it would come, would forever separate us from any further communication among our beloved people, denying any future relationship with them, including with my own siblings. The pain of such a scenario once more came down crushing upon us. It seemed we could not escape man's condemnation and we would not abandon God's call. We were in the perfect position for a miracle.

House on Sam Hill

Barn on Barbara's childhood home-Sam Hill, Penn

Barnes Hospital, St Louis, MO-first ear surgery

Chiropractic Hospital where my brothers and sister were treated.

Ben and Barbara's first home near Bowling Green, MO

Our dream house in Penn. 1983

Our barn set across a meadow.

Girod family 1995 Michigan

Idaho home under construction

Our Idaho Home

Girod family at Stephan Girod's wedding to Orpha
Miller, September 5, 2009, Libby, MT

Roman Nose mountain, Idaho

2007 Israel Mission with Global Gateway Network.
L-R, kneeling-Ben Girod, Bill Henshaw, Micah Smith

Jerusalem, Israel 2007
L-R, Amir Orly, Ben Girod

Anabaptist Connection team on the hillside just below the
Trachselwald Tower in Trachselwald, Switzerland.
Team members are From L-R around circle Mary Yoder,
Roy Yoder, Henry Yoder, Verna Yoder, Dora Girod,
Benjamin Girod, Ben Girod, Barbara Girod

A defining moment.
Charlottown, Prince Edward Island. August 1, 2002.
L-R- Geri and Lilo Keller from Switzerland, Ben
and Barbara Girod from Bonners Ferry, Idaho

Chapter 11

THE BLESSING OF OPEN ARMS

Learning life's lessons are not easy courses in God's training program. I have found however, that it is in fact during the toughest moments of maximum pressure that the greatest and most significant life lessons are learned, if one is teachable.

We faced times where the temptation to "follow the crowd" was almost more than we could bear. Like any human being, we Amish long for acceptance. Standing against the pressure of rejection was one of the most unbearable aspects to our journey.

But God was there even when we didn't feel like He was there. He never left us. We learned that Jesus wasn't ruled by people's opinions. Even His critics acknowledged his integrity and his ability to stand against the tide of human judgments.

Matthew 22:16 (KJV).

And we learned that the severe pressures of life can become emotional dark and seemingly impenetrable clouds, that envelope one's soul, reducing our ability to perceive the situation clearly. In such moments, we understood David's words, "be still and know that I am God." Psalm 46:10(KJV)

It is natural to become caught up and focused on the situation at hand, while missing the big picture of what God is accomplishing in our lives. It is only when the clouds clear away and the Sun breaks through that we realize that God was there all the time, working behind the scenes to provide and protect and preserve us.

The Bible's words through Paul often came to mind, encouraging me to remain focused and persistent. 1 *Corinthians 9:27 (KJV)*

During this time of learning and growing in Christ, God surprised us with open arms. Nearby, a small Amish community invited Barbara and I to come and live among them. They were in every sense of the word, a sanctuary of peace for our family. Not only did these people open their arms to us, they opened their hearts too, especially the senior elder, Emery Weaver. Emery, immediately supplied me with a job at one of his pallet mills in the community. This was a huge blessing for us and felt like a breath of fresh air.

We moved the twenty miles to neighboring Snyder county on a beautiful spring day in 1986. Using a team of horses and a wagon, we transported our household goods, furniture and possessions to a house we rented from one of the local farmers.

It was also a day etched with sadness, as we left our beautiful home on the crest of Sam Hill. This was a painful lesson, which helped us understand that plans do not always turn out as we expect. And as is often the case, expectations travel with disappointment. We were disappointed because once again, we were leaving the home of our dreams. Never would we return to the place where Barbara had grown from childhood.

In spite of the circumstances, we entered this new community with thankful hearts. Like guardians, Shade and Jacks Mountain, flanked the small village, giving us a sense of God's protection. Even though we did not know these people very well, the friendly faces, genuine acceptance and open arms are precisely what we needed. They will never know what their help meant to us or how wonderfully God used them to heal our sore souls.

These dear people reached out to us at the peril and cost to their own connections and relationships within their own church communities.

Emery Weaver, who was the spiritual father of the community, remained a constant inspiration to us. Among the men in my life that mentored or shielded me, he was a bright light. To my dying day, I shall be grateful for his fatherly blessing and protection.

But even as we settled into our new home, new threats against us rolled in like a storm.

It was during this time that I began appealing to a well-known Amish bishop by the name of Jacob Stoltzfus from Brush Valley, PA. I asked him for assistance in responding to the slander and false reports, which had grown in new levels of meanness and attack. For two years, I worked with him with apparent good results. The bishop himself soon understood that the false charges would never hold up in a court of law. But even so, in the end, he gave up because he was unable to cope with the pressures surrounding our situation.

Meeting after meeting was conducted in many Amish communities concerning our case. In one of these meetings, a large gathering, represented by many Amish communities in the Eastern USA, I was to be represented by three bishops that I did not know. They were to speak on my behalf. Yet, these bishops, never came and talked with me, or investigated my situation, nor asked for my testimony. Nor was I invited to attend the meeting. Still, they were called upon to represent me in my defense and were quickly overruled by the opposition. Consequently, in the end, I was condemned without trial.

It was at this time that Emery Weaver with his wife Maryann asked me to travel with them to Middlebury, Indiana, where we consulted several Amish bishops. We hoped these men would accept an invitation to travel back to Pennsylvania to help in my case, which at a later date they did accept.

I was ordained as a minister, while living in this community. Preaching the Good News of Christ to the people I loved was a joy. God helped me to navigate the murky waters of tradition as I shared the possibilities of new life in Christ. And the people responded as hearts were stirred with new hope and faith. The original Anabaptist message was fueled by the amazing grace of Christ, when he died on the cross of Calvary for the sins of mankind. John 1:29 (KJV) And just like Jesus promised, He rose again on the third day, giving salvation to every person who calls on the name of the Lord. Romans 8:11; Romans 10:13-17 (KJV)

We traveled back to Pennsylvania and it wasn't long before the fires of spiritual renewal and revival burned brightly in the small community. There were many people who came to a saving knowledge of Christ as Savior and Lord.

But the same pattern repeated itself again as a raging persecution was about to come upon my head from all directions. It was at this time that I became extremely weary of these battles that I began reasoning with Barbara about the possibility of backing off a little, and perhaps accept and acknowledge some of their accusations, as outrageous and unreasonable as they were. I reasoned with her that perhaps we could concede and confess to such charges, while at the same time avoiding denial the ways and means of the Lord working in and through us. Perhaps this act would relieve the pressures. I hoped to diffuse the ire of the leaders spearheading my ouster within the church, and the ultimate ban and excommunication.

Barbara although quiet and shy, was also a strong woman of unshakable faith. She quietly but firmly stated her position: if I wanted to acknowledge these accusations at the cost of compromising our relationship with Christ, then I may do so, but never with her consent. I was shocked and truly amazed at her gumption and boldness in standing firm in the face of such vicious opposition. Barbara's encouragement convinced me not to yield under the pressures to conform to their religious system and their religious attacks. Barbara keenly understood the extreme pressure I was under to conform. Her discernment and quiet resolve never once caused her to be concerned about the cost of such a decision. Although this season of our lives felt like we were going from crisis to crisis, the events in turn opened the door wide for our next steps in following the Lord.

When you know who you are in Christ it frees you from the need to impress others. As painful as it is to be condemned, it's far worse to give up the course God has for you just for acceptance. At some point you must ask, 'How much am I willing to lose in order to be accepted?' When we asked ourselves, "Can you take the pressure?" we were able to respond in Christ, "Yes!"

I also learned, but not for many years, that I was the crux of the problem. Not the people who resisted us. It is true that God uses the tests and pressures of life to grow us but at the same time He wanted me to find his peace in the pressures and the problems. If one only has peace when times are good and comfortable, then it is not a peace from heaven. John 14:1-5; John16: 33 (KJV)

Chapter 12

THE POWER OF FORGIVENESS

O ne day a group of young Nebraska Amish families, who lived nearby, invited me to join them for an evening of fellowship. They hoped I could answer their growing questions concerning faith in Christ. At first, I avoided their questions because I simply didn't want to add any more pressure in my life. The church leadership monitored my every move, while zealously trying to catch me evangelizing again.

By now, I was already a marked man to be avoided by the community. For a long time following, whenever I passed people during a day's routine, they often reacted with a jolt and their eyes would pop open in shock. Then they would turn abruptly, quickly fleeing the opposite direction. Others, out of curiosity would slink about, venture a question or two and then just as quickly disappear. It was mystery to me why people reacted in such a manner, yet these reactions were repeated over and over, wherever I went. Sometimes their responses would strike me as funny, other times I was dismayed. Even within the Amish system, I had not been judged as a criminal or a lawbreaker, but still the old traditions ran deep and it burdened my heart.

The young Nebraska couples were persistent in seeking Christ and they assured me that our gatherings would remain confidential and safe, so I finally agreed to visit with them. But the word got out about our first meeting and late in the evening, around 11:00

PM, trouble arrived in a fury. Suddenly, the door flew open and in walked the parents of the three young couples. And they were in an uproar, zeroing in on me with their angry words. The young men stepped between us, trying to calm down their parents. They took responsibility for the meeting, calmly informing their folks that they had invited me to visit with them. Further, they said, "Ben, is blameless in this and did not set this meeting up, we did!" But their parents never heard a word they said. They had already decided to make an example out of me by reporting this meeting far and wide.

The air in the community quickly became highly charged, as the rumor mill steadily kept grinding out and flashing the latest reports, "this deceiver", "Ben Girod is now deceiving the Nebraska Amish as well."

It was not long after this, that the gavel sounded, and the verdict was out: "guilty as charged." a community ban was placed on our family and, excommunication was final. We were shunned. Perhaps half of all the Amish churches in the U.S. honored that ban, and declared me a heretic. The stigma and shame attached to this label was overwhelming, for by now, I was a nationally known heretic. The inevitable had happened; we would now join the ranks of hundreds of other Amish outcasts before us, whose lives were shattered under a stigma of shame and suspicion never to be accepted among Amish society again!

People might present a friendly face after that, but the stigma of shunning was impenetrable. Shame now loomed over us with a wall of separation, which kept us on the outside looking in. The only family and life we had ever known was now isolated and distant, not by miles but by an age old, religious spirit of rejection. All those who had been near and dear to us in life, including most of our close relatives, even my brothers and sisters, now shunned us.

Yes, the Lord was with us, but honestly, it felt like the path became inky dark and we battled feelings of loneliness, rejection and uncertainty. This season of life continually drove us into arms of father God, who never rejects, abandons or disappoints us. We moved forward by taking one step at a time, living one day at a time, yet never knowing what the future held, but knowing God held us. But I was fully aware that our journey would not be an easy one. It must have been Three years before our challenges at Beaver Springs, Pennsylvania, while still living on our beautiful farm at Sam Hill; I had received a personal word from the Lord. The Holy Spirit used *Ezekiel 2:3-8.* (KJV) to prepare and fortify us in following Him through the trials.

In the meantime, evil reports kept circulating. Our mailbox was inundated with letters containing accusations and false reports. Somehow, the Lord held us tight in His grip of Grace and we stood firm in the face of widespread rejection. However, there was a bright spot in the ruling announcing our excommunication from the Amish Church. Resulting in spiritual shock waves throughout the Amish system. For many people, the historical traditions were now in question. We heard reports of people consciously checking the not only the validity of some traditions but also their stability to stand. It would be much later that we realized, that for the first time in generations, the Amish church was compelled to do some soul searching, and to question if their faith grounded in Christ and founded on the Bible. Galatians 3:1-5 (KJV)

Another marvelous work of God's grace was seen in a good number of people who were radically changed by calling on the Lord Jesus for salvation. Romans 10; 13; 2 Timothy 1:9 (KJV)

Young families especially noticed the change in their lives and were compelled to follow Christ. Once again, revival and renewal swept over people who were hungry for the life Jesus promised. John 7:37-38 (KJV)

This revival was reminiscent of the ones we experienced in Bowling Green, Missouri, and Snyder County, Pennsylvania. Amazingly, three consecutive spiritual revivals had been unleashed, influencing the Amish people on a national scale. I had never heard of anything like this happening before. Although, I did not wish hardship or trouble upon anyone, many Amish bishops were distressed because the seemingly immovable religious set of rules and regulations began to shake and tremble.

Due to these shakings, it would be but a matter of time when many of Amish members would not only question the validity of their system, but also begin to search out the truth on their own. As I have been able to determine through my own study, it appears that change in any religious system has always produced this kind of spiritual reform and transformation. Now, twenty-five, plus years later, one can still find a spiritual revival sweeping through many of Amish communities throughout the nation. The roots can be traced back to the small community near Beaver Springs, Pennsylvania. This was unprecedented among the Amish people and many visited the community to see first hand evidence of this transformed church. On the other hand, the bishops were faced with the reality that changes were coming to their churches, which was beyond their control. I will be among the first to state that change for change itself is not necessarily healthy or good. History teaches us that human nature swings the pendulum from one extreme to another. When people are oppressed they often move into freedom without restraint and into behaviors that are harmful and often destructive. When Jesus sets a person free, it is not a license to live and do whatever they feel like doing. It is rather a liberty to follow Jesus in a love relationship, obeying His commands because we love Him, not because we are enslaved to a code or regulation. When an Amish member violates established tradition, the Amish system of shunning was created to maintain the purity of the community and hoped to correct the apparently erring member, whereby they would be restored to the Church. But religion in and of its self is helpless to genuinely accomplish the kind of restoration that Christ offers. Religion always operates as a set of rules without a relationship. I agree that Jesus has a standard for His people. It is to love God with all of your heart, soul and mind and love your neighbor as yourself. Matthew 22:38-39 (KJV) and He does make the connection that our love for Him and our obedience are intrinsically connected, John 14:15 (KJV)

Yet, Jesus corrects us without condemning us and He certainly doesn't reject people based upon a corrective measure that is without hope of forgiveness and restoration. John 8:1-11 (KJV)

One night, we had a very rare and unusual experience. At a very late hour an outside door to our house opened and closed repeatedly, over the course of several minutes. As we considered this odd event, we concluded that God sent an angel to open and close the door, signaling us to move on through His open door. Whether an angel or not, it was the hand of God showing us that the harvest field was waiting for us, far beyond our scope or capacity to understand. Our destiny was waiting.

A couple of significant things happened at this point. First, I began contacting Amish Churches in other parts of the country, inquiring if they would agree to meet with me. I was not surprised to learn that news of the events in Beaver Springs, had reached their communities with a stir. Second of all, the six senior bishops from Indiana, Michigan, Montana and Aylmer, Ontario Canada, agreed to come and investigate the matter. When they came, they not only interviewed me, but numerous other sources as well, who were involved in the ruling to ban and shun my family. This included bishop Jacob Stoltzfus. For days, they deliberated the evidence before coming to a final decision. In the end, they found no scriptural basis for the ban so they lifted it, setting us free from the painful stigma of humiliation and disgrace.

May God reward these six bishops who traveled many hundreds of miles to come to our aid, investing time, money, and much prayer on our behalf.

Even after the bishop's decision and findings, the former opposition refused to lift the ban. Still, the bishop's help came like a wind of relief in a smoke filled room because we could freely breathe again. Although many of our relationships remained shattered, we held tightly to the Lord and He held tightly to us.

Over the next three years, we remained in the community and gladly formed new friendships. This was a huge encouragement with renewed hope.

We still longed to find and settle in a place of peace to raise our growing family and be free to share the Gospel of Christ without repudiation. Every time we became discouraged, we found hope in the Lord.

Chapter 13

CHRIST OUR REFUGE

Once again we were in a new State. It was a beautiful autumn day in late September 1989. The sadness of moving away from our friends and associates was difficult, but we now had high hopes of gaining new friendships with fellow believers in central Michigan. The countryside was full of fall color as the maple trees became draped in the beautiful hues of red and yellow. For me this was always a special time of year, especially when living on a farm as we were now doing.

While still living in Pennsylvania we had become aware of numerous scattered Amish communities in the State of Michigan where the biblical teaching of the new birth (John 3:3) was taught, experienced and modeled, beginning with following Jesus call for water baptism. Matthew 28:18-20 (KJV)

When we heard these reports we were so overjoyed at the news that a group of us traveled to Mio, Michigan to investigate these exciting reports. To my utter amazement, I found these reports to be true.

It was not often in my life that I felt such excitement combined with joy and peace. But when we visited Mio, Michigan, the holy presence of the Lord covered us in a such a generous manner; the impression of this visit still remains with me.

These dear people accepted us with the open arms of love and acceptance. The passing of time, internal testing and external personal trials had caused me to wonder if God had forsaken the Amish. I battled this fear often and it was in Mio, Michigan that I regained new hope for my people. A seeming peaceful atmosphere reigned over this community wherever I went among them. I remembered the words of David, "I had fainted, unless I had believed to see the goodness of the LORD in the land of the living". *Psalm 27:13 (KJV)*

After this, we searched out a community in Michigan to become part of this new move among the Amish. Accordingly, we were welcomed into a group in Elsie, Michigan and once we settled in our new farm of 40 acres, we felt such joy; it was tangible, even indescribable.

We had forgotten what it meant to be free, free to hold our heads up and look around with abandonment, free to enjoy life without the tension and judgment and ridicule. When I think of that moment, the best description I can come up is that we knew freedom so exhilarating that we sang like the warbling meadowlark. We had not experienced such joy since the day the Lord met us back in Missouri. It was with great anticipation that we looked forward to the sweet fellowship our new community and beyond. Rarely, did I ever bubble over with such delight and jubilation.

Having no supplemental income, which was needed at the time, I went into our local town to look for a job. I began working in the town's only lumberyard, and was soon yard foreman. I really enjoyed the work, and loved interacting with customers and was soon well known in the local community. This is where I worked for the next three years, using my bicycle for transportation for a five-mile ride each day. In addition to the job in the lumberyard, I also managed a small hog operation on our farm. Because of all of these responsibilities, which included home-schooling our children, our lives were busy. At the same time, the church community also began to grow. New families moved in who were also seeking to grow in God's word and a personal relationship with the Lord. As one might guess, this delighted me to see and be part of such inquiring and seeking hearts in knowing Jesus.

One would must understand that this kind of freedom in virtually unknown within the confines of Amish church traditions. They were in fact, revolutionary, breaking through the barriers of accepted custom. Consequently, a major reaction from the surrounding communities awaited us.

Slowly, this fledgling community began to study Jesus teachings on the kingdom of God. See Matthew 4:17, Matthew chapter 5 and 6:33, for example.

We knew there was much room to grow in Christ. We also knew, much of what we were seeking was off-limits to even some believing elements of the Amish. In fact, we soon began to realize that we were treading on some very sensitive biblical issues that went beyond the accepted tenets, even among these surrounding churches. The doctrine of the "New Birth" was the limits these churches generally tolerated, anything beyond that was looked upon with suspicion.

When it came to issues such as; being filled with the Spirit, physical healing, midweek bible studies, speaking in tongues, or prophecy, were not only off-limits, but also generally unacceptable. See Mark 10:15, Luke ch.9 and Romans 14:17 for examples.

In regard to these issues, this little community would in due time come under severe scrutiny, together with the fires of persecution for embracing these biblical doctrines.

In spite of this, we slowly and carefully, kept moving forward to new and undiscovered spiritual realms never desiring to flaunt or advertise our faith. But as of now, our community was still in it's developing stages, both in the natural and spiritual, where eventually, it would break through the barriers of legalism and the prevailing orthodoxy beyond anything seen in recent Amish history.

Chapter 14

SELF VERSUS THE SAVIOR

Little did I know, it was in this new community where God had prepared a couple, Roy and Mary Yoder, to become life long friends and partners in ministry. Over time, I saw how he proved to be a friend closer than a brother Prov. 18:24 (KJV). Before long, our connections began to develop into a trusting relationship, a relationship that in the following twenty years would be severely tested again, and again.

Nonetheless, this was when Roy and I began standing together in the what has become known as spiritual warfare. Ephesians 6:1-18 (KJV) Together, we stood under all manner of attacks, both from within and without. Roy and Mary never faltered in the grace of God. Once we linked our faith and friendship together in Christ, it withstood every round of spiritual and physical confrontation.

God's mercy over this couple cannot be overstated. I recall how many years later, Roy was close to death from a long-term illness, which caused him great suffering. Mary was alone during this ordeal and desperately held an all night prayer vigil for Roy. Promptly at 3:00 AM, heaven invaded their home. Roy didn't expect to see another day, when suddenly he got up wondering what had happened to him? All of his pain and sickness were immediately gone. There was no logical reason for this to happen. This was an undeniable miracle! Roy's time on earth was not over nor was God finished with him. God had a great deal more in store for Roy and Mary to accomplish for His kingdom.

Let me say clearly that I do not believe nor am I stating that the Amish people are evil. God loves the Amish and so do I and it is my most fervent prayer that only God's best fills and covers all Anabaptists. However, I do believe that in some cases the traditions have replaced the word of God as found in the Bible and human control has implemented evil systems that bring spiritual death rather than spiritual life. When this happens, evil spirits take advantage of the systems that man puts in place and it is those hellish spirits manipulating the man-made systems that become evil. Jesus graphically addressed this in Matthew 23.

The powers of darkness and evil are unrelenting and it is always their intention to discourage, divide and de-rail, God's plans and purpose in one's life. And such was the case now. The velocity of spiritual attacks through all manner of accusations and evil reports was rampant. However, we continued trusting the Lord and working together, resulting in this small community becoming consumed with finding the undiscovered joys of the Lord in fresh and personal dimensions. They began looking beyond the sphere of the Amish traditions which had traditionally been the religious glue holding them together. To my amazement, and despair, it would be among the believing churches in Michigan that the legalistic spirit raised its fearful dark features in a way that surpassed even that of my own Swiss environment.

History bears out that the Anabaptists started their movement under the leadership of Conrad Grebel, Felix Manz and George Blaurock. They experienced perhaps one of the greatest insurgence of Holy Spirit's power since the time of the Apostles. This movement flourished under the fires of severe persecution for two hundred years. Because of the powerful anointing following these early leaders, this revival spread over most of Europe, Russia, and eventually to North and South America. However, in the past one hundred years we have become known as "the quiet people in the land." This phrase has its roots in our history in Europe and Russia, wherein we made an agreement with their governments to lay aside our passion and commitment for evangelism in exchange for our freedom to live peaceably in the land. We abandoned the great commission. Matthew 28:18-20, Mark 16:15 and Acts 1:8-11. (KJV) My heart aches when I think that we Amish and Mennonites could completely lose our first love for Jesus. Even more troubling is what would follow if we did lose our first love for Jesus, the candlestick, representing the light of Christ would be removed. Revelation 2:5 (KJV)

This not only quenched Anabaptist's fire to take the Good News of Christ to all nations, it effectively put the fire out. As a viable people of the kingdom, we have become the "quiet people in the land". It was then and it is now my goal, to re-dig those wells of salvation and lead others to these same living waters of faith in God, which energized my ancestors. Only time would tell if I was willing to pay the price. Unknowingly, there were still unhealthy self-issues locked in my heart that needed to be crucified with Christ. These obstacles of "self" would be removed through the next several years. God removed them one at a time, and in my case, He used people around me to accomplish His work. Like sand paper taking the rough edges off a fine piece of furniture, God would sand off the rough edges of my soul.

Without feeling, thinking or believing I have any self righteous legs to stand on, I tremble when I consider that the fire and the power of God, we once possessed has long since given way to a legalistic and religious system with a strong emphasis on performance, thereby losing our former shining lampstand.

Somewhere in our movements spiritual journey, the familiar confines of form and tradition, along with a deep-seated fear of the Holy Spirit, has taken control of many Anabaptist hearts. Finding evidence of this fear, in both Amish and Mennonite churches was not difficult. As Anabaptists we began avoiding anything that appeared mystic, supernatural, or anything we simply did not understand with human reason. Such superstition has gripped our minds for many generations. What couldn't be explained or defined with the natural mind, we generally rejected.

God did not show me these errors quickly, but revealed them as time passed. It was staggering at times to discern the depth we had fallen from our true spiritual inheritance. Oh God, I pray, restore the burning first love for Jesus, of our forefathers who were gladly willing to die for their love and faith in Christ.

So here we were, among a sprinkling of Amish churches who lived out their faith beyond Amish orthodoxy but not inconsistent with Biblical truth. They believed in a personal salvation through Christ as a prelude to baptism. Beyond this however, one came under suspicion. These churches also developed a bond of outward unity wherein they could work together in harmony. They agreed upon certain codes and doctrines wherein they could flow in unhindered fellowship. At the beginning, when we first entered into fellowship with these churches, I felt sure our troubles were finally over as we surveyed this new spiritual landscape.

Chapter 15

STANDING IN THE GAP OF FORGIVENESS

Standing in the gap is the phrase used by the King James Version of the Bible, when describing the Prophet Ezekiel's call to pray for his people Israel, for protection, healing and deliverance. How this phrase and the depth of it's meaning would work through my life, would require years to understand. I readily admit, I'm still learning as God unfolds His plans for me to similarly stand in gap for the Anabaptist nation. Ezekiel 22:30 (KJV).

Had I understood what God was doing at the time, the trials and sufferings may have been more tolerable. Walking with the eyes of faith and not by physical sight teaches us to trust Him, even when it makes no sense to our human reason. It seems to me that God often withholds revelation of His ultimate design for our lives for the purposes of refining, purifying, and preparing us for His calling, so that we move in His power and wisdom and not our own. He always has a greater purpose than we can see in the moment. So in essence, the blistering trials were not only for my refining, but also for the blessing of many people. God always means it for good, even if others do not. Although I do not compare myself to Joseph, his life story as recorded in the book of Genesis is a real encouragement to every follower of Christ who has suffered any kind of injustice. Joseph was betrayed by his own brothers, sold as a slave to a band of nomads and carried off to Egypt, far and away from everything familiar and loved. He ended up working as a servant for an Egyptian official named Potiphar. Then, Potiphar's wife falsely accused him of rape, resulting in Joseph being tossed into a prison cell. In prison, Joseph helped one of Pharaoh's Chief Butlers by precisely interpreting his dream, resulting in the butler's life being spared and he was restored to his position in Pharaoh's service. Although the butler promised to remember Joseph and help him, he promptly forgot Joseph, once he was out of prison. Joseph continued to languish in a dudgeon for a long time. Finally, Pharaoh received word about Joseph's gift of dream interpretation and called for him for help with a troubling and reoccurring dream. Joseph's help opened the door to Joseph's promotion from prison to prominence in Egypt. What clearly stands out in Joseph's story is how God was with him wherever he ended up. When betrayed by his own brothers, God was with him. When he was a slave in a foreign land, God was with him. When he was a forgotten prisoner God was with him. Joseph never allowed his circumstances to define who he was and God never allowed Joseph's circumstances to carry him beyond God's blessing. In the end, Joseph remained faithful to God each step of his journey even in the most desperate moments. Afterward his looked at his brothers, most certainly thinking of all the injustice he had endured by their hands and said to them, "ye thought evil against me; but God meant it unto good", Genesis 50:20 (KJV).

Time passed, and others began to move into our new community. The freedom of worship was particularly attractive to the newcomers. We slowly but persistently moved beyond the accepted Amish orthodoxy in our worship services. Little by little we made simple adjustments like adding a midweek prayer service every Tuesday evening. It was in these meetings where the Holy Spirit began moving in mighty ways, setting people free, sick people were healed, and we enjoyed the freedom we had in God's presence.

At the onset of these happenings, news of our spiritual renewal began slowly sifting out to the other Amish communities. Without hesitation, we anticipated a joyful reaction, supposing people would celebrate freedom in Christ. Our expectations were mistaken and we were not prepared for the outcome. Even though these churches preached the Gospel and the "New Birth", we soon discovered, that some of the people held tightly to the old Amish traditions.

To my dismay, it became a repeated nightmare of our previous experiences in Pennsylvania. Apart from the loving presence of God, my wife and family, plus our new and good friends, Roy and Mary Yoder, we found ourselves isolated and misunderstood. Yet again, we pressed on, trusting in God's guidance. As we learn from Joseph, the Lord was with us even in the hardships. And He helped us to preach and reach Amish people in Indiana, Ohio and other States. For ten years, Roy Yoder and I unflinchingly preached the gospel to crowds of people across the Midwest. For over ten years, we saw hundreds, if not thousands of eager Amish seekers, soaking in the free gift of Salvation through Christ. No wonder we call it "Good News" for it transformed so many with great joy in the Lord.

One night, one of our sons rode his bike home from a prayer meeting. As he rode up to the house he noticed the large maple tree softly glowing with the appearance of being illuminated. Other children reported seeing the same thing on their way to school. Miracle after miracle encouraged us along the way.

Because of the turmoil, the youth from the surrounding communities kept their distance from our youth and community. It was a rare thing if they did visit our children, but our children never became bitter. Barbara and I are eternally grateful for each of our children who demonstrated godly patience and perseverance during those dark stormy years. Thankfully, they continue to honorably serve the Lord, and honor us as their parents. I thank God for each of our children beginning with the oldest, Esther, Mary, Cornelius, Benjamin B., Priscilla, Emily, Stephan, J. Marcus, and Josephine Eileen, whom we call Jolene. Barbara and the children were a deep source of consolation during those ten years of blessings and battles and scars were left on them too. Nevertheless they are a joyful and happy group, each walking in their unique calling and vocation. All of them are now married except J Marcus, and Jolene and we are overwhelmingly blessed with 17 grandchildren at this time.

Chapter 16

FORGIVENESS IS THE WAY
IN THE WILDERNESS

G od's ways are certainly not our ways and learning to trust Him when it makes no sense is part of growing in Christ. It wasn't long, before we were directed in a completely new and astounding direction. In what I can only refer to as a prophetic revelation, we knew that our next home would be in the Western State of Idaho.

This astonished and somewhat stunned me, for it made no sense. I could see no family benefit or human reason for moving to Idaho. But to stay where I was had no meaning either. Even so, I struggled and fiercely resisted such an untested move, thinking it foolishness and folly. What would other people think?

When God moves, He often moves with rapid suddenness. And this was certainly the case in our move from Michigan to Idaho. Barbara and I not only had the distinct revelation that we must go; it was a surprise to me that she wanted to go.

So, we began to prepare for a move west. Aside from that, I had always been impressed with the rugged beauty of the western states, especially since the time I was in Colorado with my siblings. Yet, I had not even remotely thought I would someday be living in this vast, unspoiled region of mountains, valleys, beautiful lakes, rivers, and clear sparkling streams.

We made all the preparations and finally the day arrived for our move, once again into an unknown horizon. On September

7, 2000, we arrived at the house we had purchased, in some of the most strikingly beautiful country I had ever seen. Once settled in our new home, the beauty was indescribable but I was still a broken man in many respects. Compounding the unhappiness I felt was the habit I had developed of looking back. I kept thinking of the people I had left and the land of my youth. Everything familiar was left behind. In the deepest sense of the word, I felt displaced, forsaken and removed from all that was near to my heart. Although incredibly beautiful country, it was a strange land, in the back woods of North Idaho. My heart ached and often in the night, out of the deep recesses of my soul, I could not withhold my groaning. Such was the pain and anguish I felt for the unspeakable loss.

While I was experiencing cultural shock, Barbara and the children loved it. They loved the vast and wild landscape with bountiful herds of deer, elk and moose. They even loved the fact that the surrounding mountains were filled with bear, wolves and mountain lions. All of our children immediately began exploring the many alpine trails, river bottoms, mountain valleys, canyons, and lakes in our new county. This was the adventure of a lifetime and a real dream come true. For them this was home. But of me, our first year in this new land was difficult and God continued to sand away at the rough spots in my soul. I struggled with feelings of isolation trying to make a rhyme or reason of our lives, which seemed to have lost its purpose.

We had no community and I had no friend. At least that is how I felt and even though I wasn't, I felt alone. The family was happy exploring the countryside, but I had lost my sense of identity and my soul was numbed. I dislike admitting it to you but exploring our property was even a challenge for me. There were deep valleys and high hills and I frequently feared I would get lost in this far out-of-the-way wilderness.

Our move west was His plan. Now I understand that but those early days, weeks and months challenged the very core of this Amish man's soul. Now, I look back in hind sight and understand it all to be part of God's plan in preparing us, especially me, for His purposes and not my own. Sometimes, God lovingly pry's our fingers off of emotional attachments and false identities so He can fill our hearts with the work of eternity and show how our true self is only found in Christ. In my human soul, I was learning that He not only makes a way in the wilderness but He provides everything we needed to make the journey in wholeness and health. Jesus really is the Bread of Life and we need Him daily. Exodus 16, Matthew 6:11.

Life in the way we had known it before was over and slowly, I admit, I learned to accept that and life took on, a whole new and better, perspective. God was now moving us into a far greater purpose of His life-giving plan of forgiveness. What I am learning is that His love and plan of redemption is offered to all people, especially fractured, wounded, and divided Anabaptist people worldwide.

It is true, Jesus redeemed mankind via the Cross-and His resurrection, yet redemption is an ongoing continuing work, as God seeks to heal, restore, and reconcile men to Himself, teaching His people how to partner with Him in this great plan of salvation. He captured my heart, little by little, resurrecting my spirit and gripping my soul with Paul's message of reconciliation and ambassadorship. I began to understand that we truly are the voice of Christ on earth, being His ambassadors of redemption, healing, restoration and forgiveness.

1 Corinthians 1:30 (KJV) and 2 Corinthians 5:18-21(KJV)

Shortly before we left Michigan an Elderly Mennonite pastor, Albert Zehr, came to visit me. Albert had heard of us so he came for the express purpose to encourage us. He was originally from Ontario, Canada, but was now living in Vancouver, Canada, where he was connected with the "Watchmen for the Nations Ministry". After we came to Idaho, we continued and developed our relationship, not realizing that this was my introduction in reaching beyond our Amish church culture and connections. We were ultimately invited to visit the church of Zion, in Vancouver, which we gladly did. The kind reception we received from Chinese pastor, Gideon Chui was unlike anything else I had ever experienced or known in church environments. I saw in this church fellowship that the ebb and flow of Christ's body is not controlled by nor hindered by cultural barriers but flowed freely because of them. This was the lesson I learned from

Gideon, which began to open my eyes, and broaden my view of the church. They received we Amish without hesitation or question.

We were received just as we were, Amish people, with a real history and a glorious future. This was new to us! Up until now, we had never been exposed to this aspect or facet of the body of Christ. Suddenly, we saw a picture, a model if you will of how the Church can function in harmony and unity with Christ being the center. And without fear or intimidation. This is a fulfillment of Jesus' words in *John 17:21 (KJV)*.

I cannot put into words how life changing it was for me to see, and experience these moments. I had dreamed about this kind of community church life for years and now it was on display in living. New vision and mission began stirring in my heart once again.

Chapter 17

THE GIFT OF BLESSING

Our time in Canada opened a door of opportunity that far exceeded my expectations. We were invited to join David Damian and a delegation of Five hundred Canadians on a repentance mission to Israel. This was something new and bold for our Amish culture. I thought back to my many days, while plowing behind a team of horses, I watched huge airplanes flying high overhead, trying to imagine what it would be like way up there in the sky. Now, I was about to find out first hand and the excitement within me could hardly be contained. Joined by an Amish brother from Libby, we departed on an EL-AL flight from Toronto Canada. Our destination was Israel. For ten days, we joined hands with this Canadian group in repentance towards the Jewish people. We spoke blessings on Israel, it's land and people everywhere we went, using Genesis 12:1-3 as our foundation. We joined the Apostle Paul from Romans chapters 9, 10 and 11 in praying for Israel. My heart was full, as the Lord continued to grow me by expanding His vision for our future.

Most of my life, I was keenly aware of an inescapable anti-Semitic view, by a large part of the Anabaptist people. Although I was unsure what to do about this, it weighed on my heart for years. Subsequently, this repentance mission provided healing in my heart and a plan of action for supporting and blessing Israel even further.

And with wonderful progress, we developed strong friendships as we connected with the Canadian delegation. We shall always be indebted to the "Watchmen Leadership" for accepting us and introducing us to a larger part of the church and Gods kingdom. When this happened, much of scripture began to take on new dimensions of meaning and relevance. Especially Paul's writing to the church in Ephesians chapters 3 and 4.

Another hallmark of the mission to Israel was when a gifted brother in Christ, spoke prophetically to me. In the prophetic word, the Holy Spirit firmly assured me, that my obedience in the past would result in new level effective ministry in the future. Further, that God would use me in facilitating a ministry of reconciliation among the Anabaptist people.

At the moment, I was unable to comprehend the prophecies full meaning, since I was not welcome among most Amish communities. Humanly speaking, it made no sense and I certainly could not grasp how reconciliation would come about. Yet I knew and understood, that man's impossibilities are in fact Gods greatest opportunities to demonstrate His power and majesty. So, in faith, I waited for the unfolding of Gods plan of things, as impossible as it seemed. Quickly, I discovered, that God would again prove Himself faithful, as the promises within this prophetic word were rapidly confirmed as true.

After I returned home, I reached a significant turning point in my life. While praying in our bedroom, I had a vision of Jesus. In the vision, Jesus spoke to me, saying that if I would trust Him with every request, He would bring His plans to pass. Nothing could stop His work. In the vision, it seemed I was taken into His very presence as He spoke to me in this indescribable moment! I knew and understood, that we were in Gods perfect plan, no matter what had happened in the past. Suddenly, it didn't matter that we had been through so many trials of rejection and judgment. It didn't matter that I was far from my home and people. It did not matter that people misunderstood, ridiculed or abandoned us. My depression was irrevocably broken. My soul was filled with the light of Jesus and I became alive with hope and gripped with a passion and resolve, to once again take up the His baton and move forward. I could breath again, smell the flowers, take notice of my surroundings, and begin enjoying life.

Even then, I had little understanding where all this was going to lead, but I knew and understood that something beyond my comprehension was being shaped. God was preparing us for influence outside the parameters of our Amish tradition.

God never misses anything and in His patience, He works to bring His plans to completion. Unimaginable numbers of Anabaptists were martyred during the reformation. And only God knows the amount of blood that was spilled onto European soil. Much like Abel's blood cried out to God as recorded in the Bible, I believe the cry of Anabaptist blood also has His attention.

Our opportunity for repentance is given, not because we deserve it, far from it, but because of His mercy. His redeeming work included each broken person. It includes people who feel hopeless while living fractured, and divided lives. This would touch Anabaptists on a global scale. While my heart was ablaze for this fresh vision of the Lord, it honestly left me breathless as I began watching this unprecedented vision unfolding like a wave of redemption. This is grace! And that grace is seen in the extended hand of Jesus, reaching down to Peter, as he sank in the stormy waves of Galilee.

For years, I had felt like an ominous dark cloud had loomed over us, as we walked through one trial and tribulation after another. Now, suddenly the cloud lifted off and rolled away, exposing the clear blue skies of God's love. Before us, lay a beautiful spiritual landscape, a land flowing with milk and honey, it was a rapturous moment to behold! It seemed I was being restored to my youth, the joy of the Lord swept over me in waves. How can I describe being free? I could sing and I could dance as the bitterness of the dark past dissipated and disappeared, never to return. I was a new man.

Even so, I still could not fully understand all that had happened, or what yet was about to happen, but I knew, and understood, we were walking in Gods perfect will, and HE was pleased! This was all that mattered because we were positioned for a miracle.

Chapter 18

ROOTS GIVE WINGS

A short time after this, I learned that a State Reformed Pastor from Switzerland was inquiring about the Anabaptist people in America. During a colorful chapter of his own spiritual journey and reflection, he began discovering how the State Reformed Church of Switzerland, had persecuted the Anabaptist people in the past. He discovered historical accounts of the church imprisoning people, confiscating their properties, burning them at the stake, and chasing them out of the country. This of course, he believed, resulted in their own hurt and loss of God's blessings upon their churches. For many years, the Swiss pastor carried this burden; not knowing how he and the State Church might make amends for these atrocities. Even so, many people still believed the Anabaptists to be heretics, having received their proper dues. Although the issue was highly sensitive in Switzerland, he was unrelenting in finding a way to reconcile with the Anabaptist people.

Unknown to us, God was working silently behind the scenes, preparing all the details for us to meet for the first time. The impact of this next step of forgiveness and reconciliation was remarkable. Barbara and I were about to embark on the most far-reaching assignment, of our lives. Without a doubt, this mission had an immeasurable outcome, not only for our people but many others also, igniting a global network of healing and reconciliation. We would watch in awe as our next step of faith would in due time, span many cultures, peoples, and nations.

Our entire lives had been prepared for this moment. Looking back over the years, all the times of crisis upon crisis, throughout the years began to make sense in my human understanding. Without these experiences of pain and loss, we were not prepared nor were we qualified to step into this arena. It sounds like a cliche, but it is true; God knows what He is doing and He knows how to get you and I to where we will make a difference on this planet. His ways are always above our ways, beyond the scope of our imagination. The reality of it all was like dream, I was trying to fit the pieces together, yet was unable to do so. The capacity of it remained out of my reach. Isaiah 55:8-9

It was a beautiful evening in August 2002. Distant potato fields were blooming in every hue of the rainbow and we could hardly contain ourselves because we were at an international gathering near Charlottown, on Prince Edward Island, Canada. The 'Watchman Team" were hosting a reconciliation gathering for the French and English Canadians, and for the "First Nations" people. Included in this reconciliation meeting was, a delegation of the Amish and a delegation from the Reformed Church of Switzerland. Coordinated by the Watchmen Team from Vancouver, this was a history-making summit between the Anabaptists and State Reformed Church. It was a hushed moment throughout the auditorium when Barbara and I first met with Geri and Lilo Keller.

As Geri began to speak about the atrocities that were committed by the Swiss State Church, against the Anabaptists, wave upon wave of the Holy Spirit swept over the audience. Our hearts were warmed while there was hardly a dry eye anywhere in the crowd. For three days, I saw the healing power of forgiveness and reconciliation in brilliant display.

My heart melted as Geri embraced us for the first time. Along with his son, Andreas and wife Stephanie, they humbly blessed us with deep compassion. I saw in Geri, a loving Fathers heart from God. This was something foreign to me, yet it was what I had so deeply longed to experience for so many years. These new beginnings with Geri and Lilo released healing wave upon healing wave. Only God could make this happen on a distant island, off the eastern shore of Canada.

In recent years, with God's help and blessing, Geri and Lilo started a ministry outreach they called "Stiftung Schleife". The German is difficult to translate but basically means, "to find or establish an instrument for sharpening". Geri and Lilo began to use "Stiftung Schleife", as a means to reach and disciple the Swiss, who had remained strongly independent of God and resistant to the Gospel. This ministry has genuinely sharpened many people for Jesus. It has become a kind of John the Baptist forerunner, reaching the German speaking nations and beyond. Multitudes of people are being transformed for Christ through this ministry. Their influence was also instrumental in compelling the Swiss government with its vast banking system, to restore money stolen from Jewish families during World War II.

In November 2002, their ministry brought three of us Amish couples over to Switzerland for 10 days. This would be a preliminary time of connecting and fellowship. This was also in preparation for a much greater gathering of healing and forgiveness between the State Reformed church and the Anabaptists, which would convene the following May 1st 2003.

From Winterthur, Geri took us to Zurich, showing us many of the Anabaptist sites in the city as well many other places over Switzerland. He also took us to the "Gross Munster" church where our history, faith and movement began. He showed us the actual room where Zwingli met with Conrad Grebel, Felix Manz and others to debate and study the Scriptures. This was also the location where their division and separation took place after a several years.

The day we visited the Trachselwald castle, where Hans Haslibacher was kept in prison for his faith, I stepped into the tower and immediately saw a plague on the wall about his incarceration, underneath it, to my utter surprise was the first stanza of the Haslibacher hymn, Ausbund, song number (#140). Quietly, in a low tone I stood there and sang that stanza all to myself. It was as if time stood still.

Suddenly I turned around, and there behind me in hushed silence, stood some 15-20 Reformed pastors, who were with us on the tour. They seemed to be struck with awe, that an Amish man from America could sing that hymn. Since they were not familiar with the history of Haslibacher, they appealed to me to give them the historical account. So in my ancestral Swiss tongue, I related to them the account of Haslibacher, for the first time.

When we were ready to leave, Walter Wieland, one of the local pastors asked me to come into the courthouse that was on the same grounds. Here the canton official, Martin Grossenbacher stepped forward, looked at me with tears in his eyes and said,

"I am a believer, and I know how we persecuted your people". Then he took a hold of me and embracing me said, "Will you please forgive us?" For a brief moment the atmosphere was electrified. I could hardly take in what I was hearing from this Swiss official. "Yes, of course, I forgive you", I responded.

This gesture coming from a civil official, under the shadow of a foreboding castle where our forefathers were tortured and martyred was beyond my capacity to grasp how it all came together. An official was making amends. I must be dreaming. These were amazing events that were taking place here in the land of my forefathers in the beautiful Ementhal valley.

Later, the descendants of Haslibacher presented me with an old brass ancestral cowbell that belonged to the house of Haslibacher. I also received from John Gerber and his wife, also from the Ementhal, an old hammered out solid copper dipper, which was used for baptizing purposes found in the basement of the first Anabaptist gathering house in the Ementhal, perhaps from the very early 1800's.

Chapter 19

A Legacy of Forgiveness

Hans Haslibacher was indeed memorialized by our people for his strong faith. And this impacted my family through the generations. In my ancestral history you can find the story of Johannes Schwartz, my great grandfather. He was a native of the Ementhal, Switzerland. It is said that he saw the clothes worn by Haslibacher, and also drank water from the well in Bern, where it is claimed, the water turned to blood. Haslibacher prophesied this himself, saying that the water would turn to blood at the same time of his death.

As a young Amish boy, I repeatedly heard my parents, uncles, grandparents and others relate accounts of our descendants early days in Switzerland and the Alsass. My ancestral homeland and the history of Switzerland, was kept alive, generation after generation.

Not in my keenest aspirations could I know, that someday I would stand in the land of my Swiss fathers, and be touched by the historical events of the past. It is not possible for me to verbalize or express the deep impressions and emotions that stirred in my heart. At one point, as I was standing on a wall that surrounded the court yard of the castle, overlooking the beautiful hills and valleys of Ementhal, I yelled out an ancestral Swiss yodel. This ran deep in my DNA and I wondered how long it had been since this valley had heard the songlike cry of my ancestors.

Oliver Girod was another of my ancestors who came from the Reformed Church. He was born high in the Jura Mountains, which is in the French speaking part of Switzerland.

On one occasion I was visiting the Swiss Mennonite congregation near Tavannes Switzerland up in the Jura Mountains, where many Girod surnames are still found. One of the Mennonites brothers, his name was Daniel, offered to go look for my ancestor, Oliver Girod's home place. Doubting, I went with him on this mission to find it the house. After all, Oliver had left this area in 1853. We began circling higher and higher up in the winding Jura landscape coming to a little village called (Champos) nestled in these beautiful pristine mountains. It was indeed exhilarating and breathtaking as we continued the search in the pure Swiss mountain air.

Amazingly, we not only found the place, but it was still being inhabited by the Girod family who were well aware of my ancestor Oliver, since he was born and grew up on this place. It has been my great privilege to stumble upon the history of my ancestors in this beautiful and majestic homeland.

Chapter 20

HEAL OUR LAND

January 21, 2003 dawned dark and cold in Lancaster County Pennsylvania. Andreas Keller from Switzerland had asked me to meet him in Lancaster County to meet with a group of Mennonite leaders, resulting in a dozen people gathering in the Petra Fellowship church near New Holland, Pennsylvania. Little did we know that by day's end, we were to take the first steps of releasing the gracious light of God's forgiveness.

Present in this meeting were; Lloyd and Elaine Hoover, Enos and Ruth Martin, Dr. Doe, Keith Yoder, Keith Weaver, Rusty and Janet Richards, Mark and Matt Buckwalter, Andreas Keller, and myself, along with a few others.

Our idea was to offer them an invitation to join a company of Amish to attend the "Heal Our Land Conference" scheduled in Winterthur, Switzerland, on May 1, 2003. The Swiss church sought to bring these groups of Anabaptists together for an incredible event.

Andreas made it clear, when he said, "First, We want to make a declaration and offer an apology for the severe persecution the State Church perpetuated against the Anabaptists. Our historical and past sins are a reproach against God and we want reconciliation with the Amish and Mennonites. Second, We believe our torment and oppression against the Anabaptists has prevented the blessings of

God upon our people, therefore we want to see God's favor restored upon the Swiss Church and its ministry."

At first, the gathering felt stiff and awkward and it took a while for the tense air to clear as we met each other. We were stepping into unknown territory None of us knew how to proceed or what to expect. As we cautiously moved into the discussion of reconciliation, I kept wondering,

"Could it be, that we will quit repeating history with its dark and shadowy past?" "Was this gathering for real?" "Is it possible to humble ourselves and release a new way of trust, and acceptance?" "Can we honestly look into each others eyes with out suspicion?" "Is God really the author of this meeting?"

These questions, and many more kept swirling through my mind as we warily faced each other, while pressing forward in our discussion. Like a man feeling his way along a wall in the night, we pressed on. It took both faith and fortitude to keep moving forward, for one never knew if there would be a dangerous cliff of misunderstanding ahead of us. Somehow we were able to dialogue and the ice was finally broken in our conversation.

To say I was amazed is a huge understatement, as the Mennonites generously accepted us with smiling faces. Since I came from a primitive, if not ignorant Amish background, this would have been entirely beyond the scope of my imagination while riding on a plow behind a draft of plodding horses back in Missouri!

The first seedlings of healing sprang out of our small Anabaptist gathering. Yes, a small beginning indeed, But one to produce healing of our wounds of disunity and religious divisions of our ancient past.

"Though thy beginning was small, yet thy latter end should greatly increase."

Job 8:7 (KJV). (See "Unlocking Our Inheritance" by Janet Richards, Masthoff Press, Morgantown PA.)

Let it be understood here; community healing, forgiveness, and reconciling severed relationships on this level, has little to do with coming into agreement with the many various creeds, teachings and doctrines found within all these movements. When we bring

Christ in the center of it, He Himself will resolve the differences, and as our Lord and Savior, lead in all coming to the unity of the faith. Ephesians 4

When Christ died on the cross, I was not there to make promises to serve and follow Him. He died for me anyway. It requires faith, to step out and make ourselves vulnerable to others without having assurance that we will be accepted. This small group broke the historical curse of isolation, and hiding and released the blessing of healing and acceptance, on the altar of self-sacrifice.

Almost five hundred years had passed and now, the Amish, Mennonites, and Reformed church, were once again sitting in unity, answering Jesus' high priestly prayer recorded in the Gospel of John Chapter 17.

Remarkably, this was the very day the Anabaptists first met in 1525 to usher in the Anabaptist movement in Switzerland. This was indeed a historic day in our history.

Chapter 21

THE FREEDOM OF FORGIVENESS

The great day in Switzerland finally arrived. There were perhaps a few thousand people in attendance during the three-day, "Heal Our Land Conference" in Winterthur, twenty miles outside of Zurich.

Switzerland is a small landlocked country with its scraggly borderlines looks like a keyhole on a map of the European continent. Accordingly, it has been said that Switzerland holds the key to bring back revival in Europe. I believe this prophecy to be true, both through the dedication and efforts of the ministry of "Stiftung Schleife" and through the various Mennonite efforts dedicated to bring healing, restoration, and revival to the people, families and churches in the nation.

During the three-day conference, Mennonite leaders, and bishops and leaders from the Bienen Berg seminar spoke to the conference gathering. The presence of God was overwhelming as the Holy Spirit moved on hearts of the people.

When Geri Keller was speaking, he made a declaration, which seemed to shake the vast conference hall, when he said, "You Anabaptists were right and we, the State Reformed church were wrong." His proclamation created a spiritual tremor throughout the reformed and Anabaptist church.

Some questioned the validity of his statement. Others doubted his authority to say such a statement. Even so, Geri spoke as a loving, spiritual father, unmoved by the either doubts or affirmations. Ultimately, his words released a glimmer of hope and rekindled God's dream of unity in our hearts. There was little doubt by anyone that a new day was dawning for this part of the body of Christ. God moved our hearts to a new level of faith, hope and intimacy with Him. Yes, it was for real!

On one occasion during the conference, Geri brought the Amish group, along with many other folks to "Gross Munster" church where Rudy Reich, leader of the Reformed State Church in the Canton of Zurich welcomed us. The large church was filled to capacity. Here the whole group of Amish stood in the sanctuary and sang some old traditional Amish church hymns in the very place where Conrad Grebel and Felix Manz first began their journey. As I reflected on this, I could hardly grasp the magnitude of the moment.

Toward the end of the service I was asked to speak. As I did, I stood behind the pulpit of the reformer, Ulrich Zwingli. From this pulpit, I preached and delivered a message of healing between the Anabaptists and Reformed Church through the sufficiency of the blood of Christ Jesus. The moment was full of tension, so much so, it felt tangible throughout the large building. Through my words and in our hearts, the Holy Spirit reached all the way back to the early fathers of the faith. I felt overwhelmed because I could not contain what we were experiencing in those moments of divine cleansing. It seemed, the past, present and future were somehow merging and harmonizing, with the favor of God. Unity was being birthed out of our discordant past. The conference in Winterthur broke down the wall that separated and divided the body of Christ for hundreds of years. Geri had carried this vision and mantle for a long time. Because of it, multitudes in Switzerland are now turning to the Lord.

Today, Amish and Mennonites leaders and churches are walking together because of God responded to the humility released in that conference. And the outpouring is not isolated, it is happening in Anabaptist communities everywhere. We are in a season of change, coordinated by the Holy Spirit preparing and sending Christ's church into the Harvest. Jesus made this clear in Matthew 9 and John 4.

I believe the harvest fields are being filled with called, prepared workers from Anabaptist believers. This is the fire of our fathers, going all the way back to the torch of reformation. This was their original dream and vision and how I thank God we can participate once again.

In the years since, I continue to connect with the Swiss Mennonites and leaders of the State church in Switzerland. Our continuing efforts for reconciliation now focus on the Anabaptist movement in the USA. We long for all the Amish and Mennonites to be healed and come together in unity. This vision and mission does not happen without setbacks or disappointments. We do not naively believe there are quick solutions to these historic divisions and animosities, but dedication and perseverance is beginning to pay off. And we march forward.

This has resulted in the formation of an Amish team, which I lead working in sync with a Mennonite team led by Mennonite bishop, Lloyd Hoover of the Lancaster Conference. We are pulling together to create and nurture an awareness that the bride of Christ is not divided, but one in Him.

Chapter 22

ADVANCING THE KINGDOM OF GOD

In November 2007, Micah Smith who founded and leads, "Global Gateway Network Ministry" asked me to join his team on a mission trip to Israel and Egypt. In Egypt, Global Gateway Network convened 200 leaders from North Africa and the Middle East to train them on how to share the Gospel with the unengaged people of their countries. While there, Micah introduced me to Swiss Mennonite leader, Ernest Geiser's sister and her husband, who work and serve as leaders of influence in Egypt. I will not mention their names for security reasons and their safety. I was also introduced to German Mennonite leader, John Das, who with Micah created a ministry reaching Muslim refugees in Germany and other closed countries. For four days, these leaders drank in the teaching, with the fire of the Holy Spirit, which equipped them to reach the nations.

While in Israel, I met Micah's friend and our Jewish tour guide, Amir Orly, who is also a University professor and accomplished speaker. Amir travels widely around the world teaching, when he is not in Israel guiding groups for Bible study on site. When leading groups across the land of Israel, Amir explains the biblical texts at each place you visit. In fact, every place you set your foot in Israel has some point of biblical or historical significance. I have never heard anyone bring the bible alive as Amir does, when we study together in Israel. However, because Christians throughout history have severely persecuted the Jews, he remains is a realist, as we discuss events like the Spanish Inquisition, the Crusades and the Holocaust.

For 16 years, Micah and Amir have frequently and candidly discussed Jesus and the truth of the Gospel. Although they have disagreed at times, they have connected unbreakable ties with each other. They use their gifts and skill to break down dividing walls between Christians and Jews by offering the Bible study on site in Israel, lecture tours in the USA, where they speak to churches, synagogues and civic groups. They also speak on television and on radio programs.

While on lecture circuits with Micah in the Western USA, Amir has been to our house several times over the past few years. On one occasion, Amir appealed to me for Anabaptist support for the Jewish people and the State of Israel. He is acquainted with, and has led thousands of Christians, touring the land of Israel and quickly understood that the Jewish people and the Anabaptists shared some historical similarities. We even discussed how the orthodox Jews and conservative Amish ran parallel in many religious respects. He appealed to me to bring a group of Anabaptists to Israel. However, knowing the general anti Semitic attitude and pervasive belief in replacement theology of both the Amish and Mennonites, I personally had my doubts of accomplishing such a thing. Even so, I became increasingly aware that we Anabaptists do indeed hold a key for the Jewish people, and rightly owe them an apology or our attitudes towards them. In light of this, I began asking the Lord, "what must I do?"

One night the Lord spoke to me about it. As I continued through the night to seek his face, I clearly saw an open door. In the vision, I saw the whole mission we were to take, even the steps along the way. It was with trepidation and much trembling that I stepped through that open door. From the beginning of the mission to the end, the Lord proved faithful to guide us and guard us every step of the way. It was just as I had seen it in the vision. Although it required a lot of work, God helped us, as only He can.

In November 2010 a delegation of 45 Amish and Mennonites, from five States and Switzerland, invested 7 intense days sharing a message of repentance and blessings to leading Rabbi's throughout Israel, which included the Chief Rabbi of the Western Wall. We also met with a holocaust survivor in the synagogue at Yad Vashem, (the holocaust museum) and the deputy mayor of Jerusalem.

Israeli news Channel 2 television crews followed us to many of the venues from Galilee to Jerusalem, throughout the week. Jacob Smith on behalf of Global Gateway Network also filmed the entire week and produced a video of the mission.

It was Amir Orly and Micah Smith, along with Benni de Leeuw, Managing Director, ADC Holidays in Tel Aviv that opened the doors and paved the way for the entire miraculous week of reconciliation and blessing between the Anabaptists and Israelis. David Davenports vision and prophetic word confirmed it. Lloyd Hoover took a big risk, as he encouraged other Mennonites to join us. Al and Ada Longenecker, whom I had not met before brought hope and inspiration to the whole mission. Ernest Geiser with Christian Sollberger from Switzerland added to the overall Anabaptist landscape for this mission.

Steve Lapp and the whole Lancaster Amish group brought confirmation to the people of Israel with the authenticity of our repentance toward the Jewish people. The flow, dedication, humility, and the unity of the whole group was a marvelous sight. For all of us, the mission was an expression of our love, acceptance, and repentance toward Israel and the Jewish people. The whole journey to Israel with its unfolding revelations was a heart changing experience, expanding our visions of Gods heart for both the Jew and the Gentile.

By God's sovereign plan, each one contributed to this most historic mission, not only a mission of hope and peace for the Jewish nation, a nation who is surrounded by a hostile environment, but also in restoring the blessing of Abraham, (Gen. 12:1-3 (KJV), a blessing we have lost through our rejection of Gods covenant promise to the Abraham's heirs, Israel.

The full harvest of all the seeds sown by each team member is still growing. Their participation in this history-altering mission released blessings to Israel but also displeasure for many team members when they returned home to their Amish and Mennonite communities. I also know for some, the cost was great, financially, emotionally and otherwise.... in this, God will surely reward them.

When one reads about the kingdom of God in the New Testament, I believe it is essential to understand that, Jesus was really referring to God's authority. In any kingdom, there is a King and that King has authority over his people. He protects, provides and preserves them. He also guides and governs them. Luke chapter 10 is Jesus' kingdom treatise.

For example, when he said in verse 9, "heal the sick that are therein, and say unto them, The kingdom of God is come nigh unto you." (KJV) Or verse 19, "Behold, I give unto you power to tread on serpents and scorpions, and over all the power of the enemy: and nothing shall by any means hurt you." (KJV), He was advancing the kingdom through His people, by the authority of God.

Obeying Jesus requires courage and humility to trust Him. That was certainly what I needed when He directed me to make a journey back in time, which really meant re-visiting all the former communities where we had lived previously. I was to meet, where possible, with the key leaders of these communities, especially those who had banned and shunned us in the past.

In each case, beginning in Bowling Green Missouri, I went to release a blessing and honor their leadership. When 2011 arrived almost a year had passed and I still hesitated to go on this mission. It was a frightful prospect because these communities represented the pain of rejection and loss for me, and my family.

"Had I really forgiven them? "Yes", in my head and heart, I believed I had. But now, God wanted me to face the real life emotional pain of compassionately confronting the gulf that separated us from one another. This difficult assignment was a final step in learning the full power of God's forgiveness and reconciliation. To my knowledge, this had never been done among the conservative Amish, in the face of a shunning or excommunication of members.

I finally approached my team with this proposal. I was instantly met with full agreement and approval to go on this mission.

As the plan developed, most of the team including my wife Barbara strongly advocated that I take along another person, something that seemed practical and most sensible. Yet, I had no release to take someone with me, at least not in the beginning. Towards the end of this mission, Lloyd Miller from Libby, Montana did join me.

I left alone, driving my car from North Idaho, traveling South and East, through many States. Overall, I visited more than twenty Amish communities. I met with key leaders, some of them I had not seen for thirty years. We met face to face, where I shared my heart and they listened and barriers dissolved. As I traveled from community to community, I knew and understood the key issue God was addressing in our meetings, was breaking the stronghold of dissension and divisions, so prevalent among the Amish nation. I felt Gods peace and liberty being released wherever I went. Often, I would seemingly made a wrong turn, then quickly find myself on the right road after all. The whole journey of some seven thousand miles was one of perpetual blessings with Gods favor every mile of the way.

When Lloyd Miller and I finished the journey, I knew the Kingdom of God had been advanced among our people. This was a high water mark of Gods calling on my life, for I learned again that His mysterious ways prove good and life giving. This mission of restoring and healing through forgiveness came to an end but it is an end that is really is a beginning. It is one of God's great paradoxical blessings. When I die, I live, when I humble myself, I am lifted up. When I repent, I am saved. When I forgive, I am set free. It certainly doesn't make sense to our human reason, but one thing I know, when I fully forgave the people who sought my disgrace and ruin, the one person who was most completely set free, was me.

Chapter 23

PEACE IN GOD'S PURPOSES

Once we passed the ten-year mark of living in Bonners Ferry Idaho, the Lord began speaking into my heart concerning our life's journey. Over and over, He faithfully led us through every apparent impossibilities. He always made a way with assurance and hope, where seemed there was none. When I roll these thoughts over in my mind, I am in awe and filled with thanksgiving to the Lord. God has blessed our lives, restored our losses and healed our hurts, in ways we could have never imagined. And there have been so many wonderful people along the way, who have been the hands, voice and feet of Jesus in the journey.

Psalms 119 became God's banner over us. It was a model and a place to find and live the God life. A life lived in the grace of Jesus Christ. For example,

Verses 33-40. Choosing the way of truth, together with His decrees, V-30. Always hiding His Word in my heart so I would not sin against Him, V-11. Loving His Word over and above the glitter of gold, V 127. Allowing Him to direct my steps and avoid iniquity, V-133. Praising Him daily for His righteous decisions on my life, V-164. Often crying for His help, and meditating on His Word.

V-147-148. His Word is a lamp for my feet and the light for my path. V-105. It was the completeness of His Word that I trusted, for His decrees remain forever true.

The first thirty years of my life before marriage was dedicated to my brothers and sisters, which, in retrospect were a prelude and a preparation for our life's journey. Following our marriage and encounter with the Lord, our lives were no longer ours, but were used by the Lord for good plan and redeeming purposes.

The quiet peaceful life, the average family life, that one often takes for granted, was not ours to have, even so, we found the capacity to completely submit to, and accept God's call. We are just now beginning to move into God's promise land of forgiveness and experience what it means to be free. Truly free from all the pressures life has attempted to lay upon us. Yet, we also know, God knows our past, present and future.

With a bit more understanding, we now see that He used even the bad things, the evil insults and false information in producing His plan for our lives. All the things we encountered in life, including all the things we encountered in life including all the people we met. He used it all for His glory and our good!

We are indebted to each of you, whom we met on our life's pathway. No matter what the circumstances may have been, it was Gods redemptive plan that we meet. In light of this, both Barbara and I say to each one, "God bless you!".

And we rejoice, knowing the power of forgiveness. This is what time-and-eternity is all about, to heal, restore, reconcile, and to redeem and forgive people out of life's worst and most extreme conditions imaginable.

Dear friends, the absolute sufficiency of the complete work of Christ on the Cross of Calvary and His resurrection, stand as an eternal witness to the power of His forgiveness. In this hope, we have this final and most glorious promise of meeting each and all of you in some future day, on those magnificent shores of heaven's Glory!

Chapter 24

THE ANABAPTIST VISION

Paul asked the Church in Galatia, "Have you come so far and experienced so much in Christ for nothing?" Galatians 3:3-4. (KJV)

Paul's penetrating questions compel me to probe my own Anabaptist roots, honestly and with humility, as I journey in God's forgiveness.

What is the original spiritual vision of our Anabaptist forefathers?

If anything, what did these early forefathers possess that we lack today? Is there anything we can learn from their humility, eagerness to serve Christ at all costs and ability to rapidly spread their influence to villages, cantons, and on into the whole European continent in a very few short years?

Where did this empowerment and energy come from? Simply said, I believe it flowed from the grace of God, the same grace that has led me on this journey of forgiveness and personal growth.

Amish and Mennonites over the generations have longed to recapture the Anabaptist vision. Much time in study has been invested in this area. There is a growing awareness throughout the Anabaptist nation that we must return to the Living Waters of Christ, which our forefathers drank from so freely.

History bears out that the first Anabaptists were much like the young church of Acts in the Bible.

If we look at them closely, you will see that their success was in being, not in doing. Several things mark the kingdom success of these people.

First, they were unconditionally obedient to the Word of God, as the Spirit led them from day to day. Discipleship was a natural part of their DNA as they studied the Scriptures, fellowshipped with one another and worshiped the Lord on a regular basis.

On the other hand, neither our Anabaptist forefathers nor the Acts Church possessed great credentials of formal education or training. In modern terms they were simple people, who lived simple lives, which seemed to be the very ingredient God used to spread the Gospel.

Because the early Anabaptist movement had no formal status or name, they were able to penetrate the hearts and minds of the people throughout Europe with the simple message of the Gospel. The power of God that enabled them to accomplish this under great difficulty was basis of their success, it was who they were, not their ability to argue and win a theological debate that propelled them forward with mighty influence.

I long for and pray that we as a people will turn the tide and reverse what I see as a minimum of global outreach flowing from our communities. Our codes will never be sufficient to empower us to fulfill the Great Commission. We must have the power of the Spirit of Christ, for human strength and ingenuity can never accomplish nor finish the task our forefathers began. Zechariah 4:6 (KJV)

The first Anabaptists believed so purely and confidently in the power of the blood of Christ to save the nations, that thousands of them willingly died for their faith, shedding their blood over Europe, to see the nations saved.

Their cry is a clarion call for us to impact nations as they did, following the example of Christ. Hebrews 5:8 (KJV)

Discipleship as a word and practice is a biblical mandate and part of the Great Commission. (Matthew 28:18-20(KJV) Yet, if one looks closely, the word is not generally found in our Anabaptist vocabulary, for it often gets in the way of our codes and conditions. None the Less, it is authentic biblical discipleship that will equip us for fulfilling the call of Christ.

The nations are waiting for us to fulfill the Anabaptist Vision. The path of forgiveness is before us and the Spirit is calling us to new dimensions of surrender and obedience to Christ. The nations wait for us to walk the highway of the kingdom, following Jesus, even if it leads us to far corners of the earth.

This is our call, our inheritance, and the true Anabaptist vision!

The End

Conclusion

Sadly, history confirms our Anabaptist attitude and practice of divisions, separations, and misunderstandings, which have taken a devastating toll on the emotional and spiritual lives of our people. Following Jesus on this journey has provided me a steady and sometimes steep learning curve. Sometimes I was surprised by what I learned in researching our history, beginning with the reformation in Europe. For example, the events that took place in Munster, Germany by a band of renegade Anabaptists in 1534-1535. After these centuries passing, I also discovered that these events were still a matter of contention and disagreement. It came to light through a prophetic word, which Lloyd Hoover's team confirmed.

Just as a splinter will fester and become infected if not removed, we understood that the full flow of God's blessing would not be released until this issue was addressed. We began our response by traveling to Munster on several different occasions, to prayerfully investigate the matter. We realize that only God's wisdom can give us the help we need in dealing with divisive issues such as this.

The global ramifications are varied but one great consequence for generations is we have been destitute of spiritual fathers to lead us along the pathway of forgiveness, restoration and acceptance. The mantle of a spiritual father is not merely holding to account our failures, sins and missteps.

We need spiritual fathers, with God's heart. Men, who will validate and bless us, exercising great patience. Men who will comfort and accept us with compassion, while guiding and instructing us, when we lose our way.

It is by way of the Cross of Christ that this kind mentoring is released in both leadership and followership.

Paul gives us insight when he writes, "I have been crucified with Christ; it is no longer I who live, but Christ lives in me; and the life which I now live in the flesh I live by faith in the Son of God, who loved me and gave Himself for me." Galatians 2:20 (KJV)

Christ brings all things to the light, and in His quest, for spiritual growth and understanding in our personal lives. It is on this foundation of exposure where we develop an unshakable relationship with our Lord and with others. All hidden motives and personal agendas lose their appeal in His truth and love.

Upon this foundation we discover the integrity of relationships with God and each other to overcome our historic wounds of strife and divisions. Such will never come on the strength of our human religious abilities to negotiate age-old codes, traditions or doctrines. There is a place to be found within the Kingdom where all differences vanish within the healing wounds of Jesus. This may be a largely an undiscovered realm, but one that is emerging for the end time harvest.

This rich historical inheritance will be released upon us to the extent that we leave our dark religious valleys of religious division and come under the healing wings of our Savior and into His glorious presence, for time and eternity. Malachi 4:2 (KJV)

Come join me in this journey of transformation, called forgiveness. Everyone is invited.

"Go through, go through the gates; prepare ye the way of the people; cast up, cast up the highway; gather out the stones; lift up a standard for the people."

Isaiah 62:10 (KJV)

About the Author

Ben Girod is an Amish Bishop. He and his wife have nine children and currently reside in Bonners Ferry, Idaho. For the past eight years, Ben has led Anabaptist Connections on a mission of reconciliation in the USA, Europe and the Middle East, impacting thousands of people.
www.anabaptistconnections.org

Endorsements

This book reveals more about the heart of God, his infinite passion for mankind and the mysteries of his ways then any theological discourse. Ben Girod is an example what that means that God chose the weak to shame the strong. His life is also an example how God is transforming our weakness in dignity and holiness so that deep spiritual authority is released out of old wounds, now healed. Ben is a living example that one single man can make a difference, as he stands in the gap for his Amish family. And he is standing for God's beloved nations. You hold a treasure in your hands!

Geri Keller

Geri and Lilo Keller, served as Pastors in the Swiss Reformed church for many years. They founded the "Stiftung Schlelife Ministry" in Winterthur, Switzerland, a ministry impacting the German speaking nations of Europe. Geri is a spiritual father of healing and reconciliation among Anabaptists. He is also the author of the timely book; "Father" They live in the Swiss village of Hofstetten outside of Zurich.

Ben Girod is one of God's verbs.

By that I simply mean, he is a man of action in the hands of God. A man of motion for our times. Frequently you will find passionate men and women of the kingdom paralyzed in the present because they are transfixed on "what's next" rather than "what's now". We need both. In the pages of this book, you will discover extraordinary courage and inspiration to follow Jesus because you love Him. That requires action, putting one foot in front of the other no matter what obstacles you face, challenges that confront you or pain you are experiencing. The Amish way of life has become increasingly popular in recent years. Movies, books and documentaries are becoming increasingly more common. But there is little out there on the media landscape that gives one such an intimate, first hand account of the blessings and the battles within the confines of conservative Amish culture. Without guile, Ben and Barbara Girod lead the reader into their world and offer us an example to follow. The Bible is full of such people. We needed them then and we need them now. People who step out in defiance of the odds to follow and obey the Lord.

Moses lifted his staff and the people moved.

Deborah marched into battle with Israel' armies

Elijah prayed and it rained.

Esther literally laid her life on the line for God's purpose and God's people

David ran toward the giant as he whirled his sling with skill.

A boy placed his lunch in Jesus' hands.

Peter got out of the boat.

Mary washed Jesus' feet with her tears.

The list of God's verbs is growing.

Care to sign up?

Micah Smith--founder and president of "Global Gateway Network" A ministry that has gone global--especially in developing, third world countries. Moyie Springs, Idaho

"Through the depths of brokenness and pain a powerful story emerges out of the Amish community revealing the wonder of the reality of the living God through the work of His Spirit. This heartfelt account is full of hope and gives witness to how God's plan through forgiveness, healing, and reconciliation can open up doors beyond ones wildest imagination."

Lloyd Hoover, Lancaster Conference Mennonite Bishop

It was in 2003 that I met Ben Girod for the first time, at a conference organized by pastor Geri Keller, of Stiftung Schleife, in Winterthur, Switzerland. The conference focused on a time of reconciliation between believers from the Swiss State Reformed Church and from Anabaptist denominations. During this time, I was impressed with the courage and the simplicity of this Amish bishop, to ask forgiveness from the Reformed brothers and sisters for attitudes of separation and judgment on the part of many Anabaptists.

Ben, and the other Amish believers who accompanied him, also willingly accepted the Reformers' requests for forgiveness of historic sins. Then, they humbly opened their hearts to receive the washing of their feet. Ben, along with others, has worked at bringing healing to the people of God in our country and beyond.

It should be noted that since the mid 20th century, there have been numerous requests for forgiveness on the part of the Reformers to the Anabaptists in Switzerland, but these requests were confined to small groups and were unilateral, since only the Reformers confessed faults, with comparative silence from Anabaptists. The Winterthur conference opened new dimensions: Amish and Mennonite representatives recognized their own responsibility in the historical divisions and also humbly accepted the Reformed confessions of persecutions.

This paved the way for subsequent reconciliations, including more official clarifications among the State Reformed Church and Mennonites. For example, in 2004, in Zurich, there was a reconciliation gathering initiated by the Reformed Church during The

Year Of Bullinger; during The Year of the Anabaptist in the Canton of Bern in 2007, where Ben Girod also brought a contribution to the Trachselwald gathering; and the culmination in 2009, of a three year dialogue between the Reformed churches and the churches of the Mennonites in Switzerland.

Other pathways of reconciliation still remain to be carried out by other groups in Anabaptism. They are to be accomplished with sober and prophetic hearts, and are necessary for the preparation of the Bride for the coming of Christ, the Lord. To create these moments of forgiveness and healing, God calls people who are pioneers like Ben Girod, who are willing to forge a new path and to pay the price of obedience.

Ernest Geiser, *Mennonite Pastor at Tavannes, Switzerland*

At Winterthur in 2003, and at Trachselwald in 2007, my meetings with Ben Girod and other Amish brothers and sisters were brief, consisting of loving looks and the exchange of brotherly or sisterly smiles. However, during the closing worship of the open-air gathering at Trachselwald in 2007, three of us were invited to participate in the serving of the communion elements. Ben Girod represented the Amish, another person represented the Reformed Church and I was invited to represent the Mennonites in Switzerland. During this time of presiding over communion, as well as during the time that followed the worship that day, I felt that God was inviting us to get to know each another in a deeper way.

So we extended to Ben an invitation to come to Switzerland. It was in 2008 that Ben Girod, along with Roy and Mary Yoder, came to visit the Swiss Mennonites. Together, we shared in the experience of visiting several Swiss Anabaptist locations: the Anabaptist training center at Bienenberg; Mennonite archives in Jeangui; sites in the Bernese Jura mountains that served as hiding places during previous times of persecution; and visiting the local church community in Tavannes (BE). Our visit created the pathway toward the restoration of Amish-Mennonite relations with Switzerland. We experienced a time of prayer we believe was prophetic, in Langnau, where three hundred and twenty years ago, a conflict occurred between Hans Reist and Jakob Amman (1693) that led to the Amish-Mennonite schism.

Following their Swiss visit, times of fellowship have since occurred between our Swiss community and the Amish community where Ben gives leadership, creating greater restoration and brotherly love by the invitation of our heavenly Father: an invitation that Ben Girod responded to with courage and perseverance.

Christian Sollberger, *Mennonite pastor in Tavannes (Switzerland)*

Ben Girod passionately desires one thing—revival at any cost. Having been born and raised Amish, he is well aware of the Anabaptist movement that took place in Switzerland during the 1500s. Who would've ever dreamed that one day that unstoppable and bloody movement would come full circle and be turned back to no movement at all—just silence and darkness?

In this book, you will learn first-hand how God has called a special man in our generation, Ben Girod, out from amidst the darkness and given him a determination and overwhelming burden to re-light the fires of revival, regardless of the cost.

Joe Keim, Executive Director of Mission to Amish People, **PO Box 128 Savannah, OH 44874**

Jesus came down from Heaven and as man walked the path of true reconciliation all the way to the finish line which, ending at the cross. In like manner Father God called Ben Girod to follow the express example of His dear Lord and Savior Jesus Christ.

When God called Ben and Barbara over 30 years ago from among the most traditional Swiss Amish, little did they know what kind of sacrifice they would make to answer the call of being Christ's Ambassador. It was a call to lay down their lives so others can live.

I consider it a great privilege to walk in the shadow of Ben Girod. Therefore I recommend this book, especially for our Anabaptist family. In it you will discover a desire to be free in Christ, to openly embrace, respect and to bless the life of Christ in others. Therewith tearing down century old strongholds, walls of divisions and replacing them with restored relationships.

Frank Thiessen
Winkler, Manitoba